SCOTTISH CATHOLICS
AT HOME
AND ABROAD

1680-1780

BY
DAVID DOBSON

CLEARFIELD

Printed for
Clearfield Company
by Genealogical Publishing Company
Baltimore, Maryland
2010

ISBN 978-0-8063-5492-7

Made in the United States of America

CONTENTS

INTRODUCTION

The Scottish Reformation was relatively bloodless and swift, and by the late seventeenth century the majority of the one million Scots had converted to Protestantism. Those who remained Catholic were thought to be fewer than 25,000, mostly located in remote areas of highland Aberdeenshire and Inverness-shire. Some others could be found in Lowland areas, particularly Dumfries and Galloway. Many lived under the protection of a Catholic nobleman or landowner, notable among whom were the Duke of Gordon in Aberdeenshire and the Earl of Nithsdale in Dumfries-shire. With the return of the Stuart monarchy in 1660, a period known as The Restoration, King Charles II allowed freedom to worship. This situation changed when he was succeeded by his brother, King James VII (James II of England), who was a committed Catholic and seen to favor Catholicism, leading to his forced exile in 1688, and an invitation to his sister, the Protestant Mary, and her husband, William of Orange, to occupy the thrones of Scotland, England and Ireland.

The adherents of the House of Stuart, generally known as Jacobites (after James VII), were sometimes considered to be a Fifth Column, prepared to support France and the restoration of the Stuart monarchy. These attempts were famously made in the Jacobite uprisings of 1715 and 1745. Recent research has brought up the perhaps surprising fact that only one fifth of the Jacobites who fought for Bonnie Prince Charlie in 1745-1746 were Catholic. Others were Protestant Episcopalian, ruled by Bishops but not recognising the authority of the Pope. Fresh penal laws were introduced in 1700 which caused the Catholic church to be driven underground, with the result that there are few records which identify Scottish Catholics of the period. In practice these Penal Laws were rarely enforced after 1730 except for a brief period after the 1745 Rebellion.

Religion was certainly one factor in the decision of many to emigrate to America. A well-known example of this was the attempted forced conversion to Presbyterianism of the residents of South Uist by their landowner in 1772, causing mass emigration to Prince Edward Island. Other Catholic settlements were established, such as Arisaig, Nova Scotia in 1793, with emigration to these encouraged by priests. It must be considered also that many Highland soldiers, demobbed after 1763 and 1783, would have been Catholic. The Fraser Highlanders, originating in mainly Catholic Inverness-shire, would be a case in point.

The period of the Clearances, starting in the late eighteenth century, saw Catholic Highlanders emigrating to North America as part of an organised mass migration. The voyage of the Alexander of Greenock from South Uist to Prince Edward Island in 1772, was closely followed by the Pearl from Fort

William in 1773 bound for New York. Later Catholic Highlanders were drawn to settlements on Nova Scotia, especially Cape Breton and Prince Edward Island, because there they could maintain their Gaelic culture and practice their religion. As illustration, the names of three shiploads of Catholic Highlanders bound for North America are included in this work.

While those who emigrated to America, for the most part remained there, others, who travelled east, did so for various reasons and sometimes returned home. After the Reformation many Catholic families sent their sons to the continent for an education, some of whom were destined for the priesthood. The main colleges for the priesthood were The Scots College in Paris, The Scots College in Douai, The Royal Scots College at Salamanca, and The Scots College in Rome. The Benedictine Abbey of Ratisbon in Germany was also an establishment which educated Scots abroad. One clandestine college in Scotland, the seminary at Morar, was disbanded after the 1715 Rebellion. Relocated to Scalan in Banffshire, this was burned down after the 1745 Rebellion. The registers of the Scots Colleges abroad identify Scottish students of the period, and these have been included in this work.

The penal laws, which restricted Catholics in Scotland, ended in 1793 and from this date church registers began to be kept. Unlike the registers of the Church of Scotland, most of which date from the seventeenth and eighteenth centuries, only four Catholic parish registers pre-date 1780; namely Braemar from 1608, Kirkconnel from 1730, Ballater from 1769, and St Mary's, Edinburgh, from 1777. Sourced from records located at home and abroad, it is hoped that this compilation of Scottish Catholics of the period 1680 to 1780 goes some way to assist the individual researcher. The best single source in Scotland for research into Scottish Catholic ancestry is the Scottish Catholic Archive in Edinburgh.

REFERENCES

HBRA =   Hudson Bay Records Archives

IR   =   Innes Review, series, Edinburgh

NA   =   National Archives, London

NAS =   National Archives of Scotland, Edinburgh

NLS =   National Library of Scotland, Edinburgh

NRAS=   National Register of Archives, Scotland

PAPEI =   Public Archives, Prince Edward Island

RPCS =   Register of the Privy Council of Scotland

RSC =   Records of the Scots Colleges, Aberdeen, 1906

SCA =   Scottish Catholic Archives, Edinburgh

SCP =   The Scots College in Paris, 1603-1792, B.M.Halloran

SF   =   Scots in Franconia, M. Dilworth

SIG =   Scots in Germany, T.A.Fischer

SNQ =   Scottish Notes and Queries, series

SCOTTISH CATHOLICS

AT HOME AND ABROAD,

1680-1780

ABERCROMBIE, ALEXANDER, of Auquhouse, Aberdeen, 1704/1705. [NAS.CH1.2.5.2/155]

ABERCROMBIE, ALEXANDER, master of the household of the Marquess of Huntly, parish of Bellie, 1710. [NAS.CH1.2.29.3]

ABERCROMBIE, JOHN, a merchant in Edinburgh, a prisoner in Edinburgh Tolbooth, released in 1690. [RPCS.XV.590/610]

ABERCROMBIE, JOHN CHRISTIAN, born 1641, educated at Wurzburg and Ratisbon, a priest imprisoned in Aberdeen Tolbooth in 1690, died in Scotland, 1714. [RPCS.XVI.469][SF.280]

ABERCROMBY, PATRICK, born 1671, son of Alexander Abercromby of Fetterneir, a student at the Scots College at Douai, 1685. [RSC.I.58]

ABERCROMBY, WALTER, at Ratisbon, 1713. [SIG#294][RSC.I.250]

ABERCROMBIE, ..., a brewer in Duddingston, Midlothian,1703. [NAS.CH1.2.5.2/151]

ABERNETHIE, ..., a priest in Aberdeen, 1714. [NLS.ms976.143]

ABERNETHY, ALEXANDER, educated at Ratisbon 1719, died in America. [SIG.294][RSC.I.251]

ABERNETHY, JOHN, educated at Ratisbon, 1718. [SIG.294][RSC.I.250]

ACHAMACHY, ALEXANDER, tenant in Bray's, with his wife Margaret Reid, and sons Alexander, George, James, and John, parish of Bellie, 1710. [NAS.CH1.2.29.3]

ADAM, JANET, in Traquair, Dumfries-shire, 1703. [NAS.CH1.2.5.1]

1 |

ADAM, ROBERT, in Robestoun, Kinnoir parish, 1710. [NAS.CH1.2.29.3/210]

ADAMSON, GEORGE, a priest on Deeside from 1703 until his death in 1707. [IR.LV.206]

ADAMSON, JAMES, a tailor in Marling's Wynd, Edinburgh, 'a papist' in Tron Kirk parish, Edinburgh, 1703/1704/1705. [NAS.CH1.2.5.2.149/151/ 175/1]

ADAMSON, MARY, with her children Robert, aged two, and Laurence, aged one, in Echt, Aberdeenshire, 1704, 1710. [NAS.CH1.2.5.3.194; CH1.2.29.3]

ALANACH, JAMES, and his wife, in Achintoul, Tullich, Aberdeenshire, 1718. [NAS.CH1.2.7.271]

ALANACH, JOHN, and his wife, Tullich, Aberdeenshire, 1718. [NAS.CH1.2.7.271]

ALEXANDER, CHARLES, from Edinburgh, educated at Ratisbon 1739. [SIG.294]

ALEXANDER, Dr JOHN, and his son John, 'papists' residing in Tronkirk parish, 1703, North Leith parish, Edinburgh, 1704. [NAS.CH1.2.5.2.149]

ALEXANDER, MARJORIE, daughter of John Alexander MD, and his wife Elizabeth Turner in St Nicolas parish, Aberdeen, was baptised by Robert ..... a Jesuit, on 17 August 1688, godfather was Alexander Menzies of Buckie, and the godmother was Mrs Marjorie Forbes, lady dowager of Pifodels. [SNQ.VIII.181]

ALEXANDER, PATRICK JOHN, born 1658 in Aberdeen, ordained in Wurzburg in December 1679, died 25 May 1682. [AF#281]

ALEXANDER, ..., a priest in Banffshire, 1710. [NAS.CH1.2.29.3/210; CH1.2.30/1/5]

ALLAN, ALEXANDER, a flaxdresser in Keith, Banffshire,1794. [NAS.SC2.72.4]

ALLAN, JAMES, and Janet Jessiman, in Mortlich, Ruthven, Strathbogie,1710. [NAS.CH1.2.29.3/209]

ALLAN, JAMES, a student at the Scots College at Douai, 1793. [IR.LVIII.223]

ALLAN, JOHN, in Shaw of Kirkconnel, Dumfries-shire, 1703. [NAS.CH1.2.5.1]

ALLAN, JOHN, tenant in Townhead of Kirkconnel, Dumfries-shire, 1703. [NAS.CH1.2.5.1]

ALLAN, JOHN, and Janet Stable, in Mortlich, Ruthven, Strathbogie, 1710. [NAS.CH1.2.29.3/209]

ANDERSON, ALEXANDER, of Tynnet, and son Francis, parish of Bellie, 1710. [NAS.CH1.2.29.3]

ANDERSON, ALEXANDER, the younger of Tynnet, with his wife Jean Lyall, in Tullo, Parish of Bellie, 1710. [NAS.CH1.2.29.3/211]

ANDERSON, CHARLES, a catechist in Aberdeenshire, 1720. [NLS.ms68.31-32]

ANDERSON, DAVID, a weaver in West Kirk parish, Edinburgh, a 'papist', 1704. [NAS.CH1.2.5.2.149]

ANDERSON, HELEN, spouse to John Begg in Braeradock, Aboyne or Glentanar, 1710. [NAS.CH1.2.29.3]

ANDERSON, ISOBEL, in Achinhalrig, parish of Bellie, 1710. [NAS.CH1.2.29.3]

ANDERSON, JAMES, tenant in Upper Achinroth, with his wife Elspet Guthrie, and son James, in the parish of Bellie, 1710. [NAS.CH1.2.29.3/211]

ANDERSON, JAMES, tenant, with his wife Margaret Kemmie, and daughter Helen, in Cottonhill, Parish of Bellie, 1710. [NAS.CH1.2.29.3/211]

ANDERSON, JOHN, tenant in Bayrs, with his mother Janet Collie, and his daughter Margaret, in the Parish of Bellie, 1710. [NAS.CH1.2.29.3/211]

ANDERSON, JOHN, of Teinet, educated at Ratisbon 1748. [SIG.295][RSC.I.252]

ANDERSON, MARGARET, wife to Alexander Dunbar in Nether Dallachie, with their grandchild Margaret Godsman, in the parish of Bellie, 1710. [NAS.CH1.2.29.3/211]

ANDERSON, MARY, servant to Alexander Tod in Nether Dallachie in the parish of Bellie, 1710. [NAS.CH1.2.29.3/211]

ANDERSON, PETER, and spouse Elizabeth Kerr, with his son John and three daughters in Charleston, Aboyne or Glentanar, 1710. [NAS.CH1.2.29.3]

ANDERSON, WILLIAM, a servant in Drumgask, Aboyne or Glentanar, Aberdeenshire, 1704. [NAS.CH1.2.5/190]

ANDERSON, PATRICK, hostler in Charleston, Aboyne or Glentanar, Aberdeenshire, his spouse Christian Ker, and children John and Anne, 1704. [NAS.CH1.2.5/190]

ANDERSON, WILLIAM, a farmer in Pittendrioch, Aberchirder, 1710, 'who converted to popry some ten or twelve years ago when he was a servant to the deceased Lord Oliphant'. [NAS.CH1.2.29.3]

ANGEEL, Mrs, late servant to Lady Roslin in Edinburgh, 'a papist' living in George Weir's Close at the head of the Canongait, later in College Kirk parish, Edinburgh, 1704/1705. [NAS.CH1.2.5.2.149;175/1]

ANGELIE, Mrs, in Watson's Land, College Kirk parish, Edinburgh, 1703. [NAS.CH1.2.5.2/151]

ANGELL, HENDERETTA, gentlewoman to Dame Anna Douglas, in Collinton, Edinburgh, 1703. [NAS.CH1.2.5.2]

ANGIER, HENRIETTA, servant to Lady Comiston, in Edinburgh, 'a papist' residing at the foot of Bell's Wynd, Old Kirk parish, Edinburgh, 1704/1705. [NAS.CH1.2.5.2.149; 175/1]

ANGIER, MARGARET, in College Kirk parish, Edinburgh, 1703. [NAS.CH1.2.5.2/151]

ANNAND, MARGARET, daughter of John Annand, in the parish of Bellie, 1710. [NAS.CH1.2.29.3/211]

ANNAND, MARGARET, daughter of Walter Annand, a tenant in the Parish of Bellie, 1710. [NAS.CH1.2.29.3/211]

ARBUTHNOTT, BENEDICT, born 5 March 1737, Abbot of the Monastry of St James at Ratisbon in 1776, died 19 April 1820. [St James MI, Ratisbon]

ARBUTHNOTT, CHARLES, educated at Ratisbon 1748. [SIG.295][RSC.I.252]

ARROT, ANDREW, of Foffartie, 'a papist' in Angus, and his wife, 1704, 1705. [NAS.CH1.2.5.3.204; CH1.2.5.2.171]

AUCHENLECK, HUGH, at Ratisbon, 1719. [SIG.294][RSC.I.251]

AUCHMUTIE, Mrs ISABEL, in College Kirk parish, Edinburgh, 1703. [NAS.CH1.2.5.2/151]

AUCHMUTIE, Mrs JANET, in College Kirk parish, Edinburgh, 1703. [NAS.CH1.2.5.2/151]

AUCHMUTIE, Mrs MARY, who washes and keeps a school in Chalmers Close, Edinburgh, 'a papist' in College Kirk parish, Edinburgh, 1703/1704/1705. [NAS.CH1.2.5.2.149/151/171]

BADHAM, Mrs, the elder, a schoolmistress, and her grandchild Susanna Johnston, in College Kirk parish, Edinburgh, 1703. [NAS.CH1.2.5.2/151]

BADENOCH, ALEXANDER, a student at the Scots College at Douai, 1793, later rector of the college at Aquhorties. [IR.LVIII.223]

BAGNALL, THOMAS, a student at the Scots College at Valladolid, 1787, later at New Abbey, Galloway, died 27 May 1826. [RSC.I.210]

BAILLIE, ALEXANDER, born 1668, son of Alexander Baillie of Shirill, a student at the Scots College at Douai, 1682. [RSC.I.56]

BAILLIE, ANNA, servant to Lady Pitfodell, in College Kirk parish, Edinburgh, 1703. [NAS.CH1.2.5.2/151]

BAILLIE, BERNARD, from Stirling, at Ratisbon Monastery from 1691, died in 1743. [SIG#293]

BAILLIE, FRANCIS, a surgeon in Kirriemuir, Angus, 1704. [NAS.CH1.2.5/204]

BAILLIE, JOHN, born 1669, son of Alexander Baillie of Shirill, a student at the Scots College at Douai, 1682. [RSC.I.56]

BAILLIE, MARY, servant to Lady Jean Semple, in Edinburgh, 'a papist' living in Main's land immediately below the Half-Moon, College Kirk parish, Edinburgh, 1704/1705. [NAS.CH1.2.5.2.149/171]

BAILLIE, WILLIAM, of Carnbrae, parish of Bothwell, 1683. [RPCS.VIII.646]

BAIN, ANDREW, in Boreland, Auchterarder, Perthshire, 1703. [NAS.CH1.2.5.2]

BAIN, DONALD, with his wife, in Ardach, in Glenmuick, Tullich, and Glengarden, Aberdeenshire, 1718. [NAS.CH1.2.47/284]

BAIN, or GRANT, MARGARET, spouse to Patrick Stuart in Inverastry, and their son John Stuart, Strathaven, Banffshire, 1708. [NAS.CH1.2.30/1/28]

BALLANTYNE, JOHN, sometime one of the Gentlemen of the Guards, in bailie Rae's land at the head of the Canongait, 1704; 'a papist' in Canongait, Edinburgh, 1705. [NAS.CH1.2.5.2.149/170]

BALMANNO, ALEXANDER, in Blairhead, Cargill, Perthshire, and two children, 1704. [NAS.CH1.2.5.3.203]

BANNATYNE, JOHN, late one of the Gentlemen of the Guard in bailie Rae's Land at the head of the Canongait, Edinburgh. 1704, 1705. [NAS.CH1.2.5.2/149, 154]

BARBER, JOHN, a shoemaker, with his sons James and John, parish of Bellie, 1710. [NAS.CH1.2.29.3]

BARBER, MARGARET, a servant in Fochabers, 1710. [NAS.CH1.2.29.3/210]

BARCLAY, ANDREW, at the Raws of Huntly, Dunbennan parish, 1710. [NAS.CH1.2.29.3/210]

BARCLAY, BESSIE, "who teaches children popish prayers" in Fochabers, 1710. [NAS.CH1.2.29.3/210]

BARCLAY, GEORGE, servant to Mr Wauchop, a 'papist' in Liberton, Edinburgh, 1704. [NAS.CH1.2.5.2.149]

BARCLAY, JAMES, at the Raws of Huntly, Dunbennan parish, 1710. [NAS.CH1.2.29.3/210]

BARCLAY, WILLIAM, in Robestoun, Kinnoir parish, 1710. [NAS.CH1.2.29.3/210]

BARTLE, JAMES, a shoemaker, with his wife Margaret Davidson, and children James, John, and Isobel, in Fochabers, 1710. [NAS.CH1.2.29.3/210]

BARTLE, JOHN, a farmer in Fochabers (?), with his wife Margaret Davidson, and sons James and John, Morayshire, 1705. [NAS.CH1.2.5/2]

BEATON, MALCOLM, in Canloid, Arisaig, Inverness-shire, 1703. [NAS.CH1.2.5.2]

BEATON, NEAL, educated at the Scots College in Paris from 1702 to 1704. [SCP#213]

BECK, JAMES, in Dalbeattie, Orr, Dumfries-shire, 1705. [NAS.CH1.2.5/156]

BECK, JOHN, in Dalbeattie, Orr, Dumfries-shire, 1705. [NAS.CH1.2.5/156]

BECK, MARY, in Dalbeattie, Orr, Dumfries-shire, 1705. [NAS.CH1.2.5/156]

BELL, NICOLAS, in Colvend, Dumfries, 1704. [NAS.CH1.2.5.2]

BENNETT, JOHN, tenant in Nether Badfeure, and his wife Elspet Hird, in the parish of Bellie, 1710. [NAS.CH1.2.29.3]

BENNETT, MARJORIE, wife to George Geddes, in the parish of Bellie, 1710. [NAS.CH1.2.29.3]

BENNETT, PETER, tenant, with his wife Janet Kemmie, in Cottonhill, Parish of Bellie, 1710. [NAS.CH1.2.29.3/211]

BERNARD, Mrs, a housekeeper at Gordon Castle, Morayshire, 1705. [NAS.CH1.2.5/187]

BIRNEY, WILLIAM, son of John Birney, a mason in Angus, and his wife Janet Watson, was baptised by Father Robert Francis on 24 February 1690. [SNQ.VIII.181]

BLACK, JOHN, with his spouse Margaret Hannay, and children Janet and John Black, in Dalbeattie, Orr, Dumfries-shire, 1705. [NAS.CH1.2.5/156]

BLACK, MARGARET, sister of John Black above, in Dalbeattie, Orr, Dumfries-shire, 1705. [NAS.CH1.2.5/156]

BLACK, MARGARET, an apostate in Aboyne or Glentanar, 1710. [NAS.CH1.2.29.3]

BLACK, MARJORY, Parish of Bellie, 1710. [NAS.CH1.2.29.3/211]

BLACK, WILLIAM, a gardener in Barnhill, Banff, 1794. [NAS.SC2.72.4]

BLACK, ..., a priest in the Presbytery of Dingwall, 1707. [NAS.CH1.2/30/1/4]

BLAIR, JAMES, of Lethenty, son of George Blair of Pittendreich, 1690. [RPCS.XV.135/474]

BLAIR, or HEPBURN, JAMES, at the Monastery of Ratisbon around 1667, died at Monte Cassino on 1 October 1702. [SF#280]

BLAIR, JAMES, a periwig-maker, 'a papist' in Gray's Close, College Kirk parish, Edinburgh, with his spouse Bessie Corbie, and daughter Magdalen Blair, 1703/ 1704/1705. [NAS.CH1.2.5.2.149; 151/175/1]

BLAIR, ..., a maid at Balnacraig, Aboyne or Glentanar, 1710. [NAS.CH1.2.29.3]

BODDAM, Mrs, relict of ...... Boddam a schoolmaster, in Dickson's Close, Edinburgh, 'a papist' in College Kirk parish, formerly in Tron parish, Edinburgh, 1704/1705. [NAS.CH1.2.5.2.149;175/1]

BOSWEL, BARBARA, wife of James Strachan of Kainacoil, Glenmuick, Aberdeenshire, 1718. [NAS.CH1.2.47.271]

BOWER, ALEXANDER, of Kincaldrum, 'a papist' in Angus, and his wife, 1704, 1705. [NAS.CH1.2.5.3.204; CH1.2.5.2.171]

BOWER, ALEXANDER, of Easter Methie, 'a papist' in Angus, and his wife, 1704, 1705. [NAS.CH1.2.5.2.171; CH1.2.5.3/204]

BOWER, ALEXANDER, son of Alexander Bower of Methie, Angus, educated at the Scots College in Paris, 1748. [SCP#217]

BOWER, FRANCIS, son of Alexander Bower and Carol Starlin in the diocese of Brechin, educated at the Scots Colleges in Paris and in Rome from 1704 to 1711. [SCP#213]

BOWER, ..., of Kincaldrum, Angus, a resident of Dundee, 1782. [IR.XVII.77]

BOWYER, FRANCIS, born 1683, schoolmaster at Morar, Inverness-shire, a Jacobite transported from Tilbury to the West Indies on 20 March 1747. [P.2.44]

BOYD, CHARLES, son of the Earl of Kilmarnock who was executed as a Jacobite in 1746, died in Edinburgh on 3 August 1782. [IR.XVII.49]

BOYN, MARGARET, a servant in Fochabers, Morayshire, 1705.
[NAS.CH1.2.5/187]

BRADFOOT, GEORGE, son of Daniel Bradfoot, a student at Douai, 1750.
[RSC.I.87]

BREMNER, ADAM, son of Robert Bremner, and his wife Margaret Stuart, in the
parish of Bottarie, Strathbogie, 1710. [NAS.CH1.2.29.3/209]

BREMNER, ANDREW, in Ryfinn, parish of Bellie, 1710. [NAS.CH1.2.29.3]

BREMNER, ARTHUR, son of Robert Bremner, and his wife Janet Brown, in the
parish of Bottarie, Strathbogie, 1710. [NAS.CH1.2.29.3/209]

BREMNER, JANET, in Fochabers, 1710. [NAS.CH1.2.29.3/210]

BREMNER, JOHN, tenant in Cottonhill, with his daughters Janet and Marjory, in
Cottonhill, Parish of Bellie, 1710. [NAS.CH1.2.29.3/211]

BREMNER, ROBERT, in Ordbrae, with his wife Margaret Geddes, in the parish
of Bottarie, Strathbogie, 1710. [NAS.CH1.2.29.3/209]

BRIDGE, JANET, servant to Thomas Maxwell in Kirkconnel, Dumfries-shire,
1703. [NAS.CH1.2.5.1]

BROCKIE, MAR., from Edinburgh, at Ratisbon Monastery from 1708, died 1739.
[SIG.293]

BROWN, CATHERINE, wife of Gilbert Knight, in Fochabers, 1710.
[NAS.CH1.2.29.3/210]

BROWN, ELSPET, at the Raws of Huntly, Dunbennan parish, 1710.
[NAS.CH1.2.29.3/210]

BROWN, GEORGE, a 'papist' in the Canongait Tolbooth, Edinburgh,1703/1704/
1705. [NAS.CH1.2.5.2/149/151/ 170]

BROWN, HUGH, a surgeon in Edinburgh, an apostate and 'a papist' residing
near the Tolbooth, New North Kirk parish, Edinburgh,
1704/1705.[NAS.CH1.2.5.2.149/154/175/1]

BROWN, HUGH, son of Hugh Brown a surgeon, and his spouse Elizabeth Hamilton, in Edinburgh, 'papists' in Grayfriars Kirk parish, Edinburgh, 1705. [NAS.CH1.2.5.2.175/1]

BROWN, or CONSTABLE, JAMES, from East Fortune, at the Ratisbon Monastery from 1698, died 1720. [SIG#293]

BROWN, JAMES, an apostate and a 'papist', son of Hugh Brown a surgeon, and Elizabeth Hampton his wife, an English woman, and their daughter Margaret aged 2 years, in Greyfriars Kirk parish, Edinburgh, 1704. 'Their nearest Protestant relative is Robert Campbell a surgeon who is married to his sister'. [NAS.CH1.2.5.2.149/154]

BROWN, JANET, in Richorne, Orr, Dumfries-shire, 1705. [NAS.CH1.2.5/156]

BROWN, JOHN, born 1684, son of the laird of Nountoun and Agnes Maxwell, a student at the Scots College at Douai, 1698. [RSC.I.65]

BROWN, JOHN, in Fochabers, Morayshire, 1705. [NAS.CH1.2.5/2]

BROWN, JOHN, tenant, Parish of Bellie, 1710. [NAS.CH1.2.29.3/211]

BROWN, KATHERINE, in Fochabers, Morayshire, 1705. [NAS.CH1.2.5/2]

BROWN, HELEN, spouse to Thomas Henry, in Edinburgh, 1703. [NAS.CH1.2.5.2]

BROWN, JOHN, a tenant, with his wife Margaret Moor, also children Jean and Margaret, in Fochabers, 1710. [NAS.CH1.2.29.3/210]

BROWN, KATHERINE, wife of Gilbert Crighton, in Fochabers, Morayshire, 1705. [NAS.CH1.2.5/187]

BROWN, MARGARET, in Auchterarder, Perthshire, 1703. [NAS.CH1.2.5.2]

BROWN, ROBERT, of Bishopton, his spouse Bethia Maxwell, and children Gavin, Gilbert, Winifred, and Agnes, in Milnehead, Kirkmahoe, Dumfries-shire, 1705. [NAS.CH1.2.5.1]

BROWN, ROBERT, son of Robert Brown of Millhead and Elizabeth Maxwell, a student at the Scots College in Madrid, 1721. [RSC.I.200]

BROWNHILL, ROBERT, and his wife Elizabeth Miln, with an infant, a tenant in Athelstoneford, East Lothian, 1703. [NAS.CH1.2.5.1]

BRUCE, GEORGE AUGUSTINE, born near Edinburgh in 1659, entered the Wurzburg Monastery in 1677, died in 1716. [SF#280]

BRUCE, JAMES, from Clackmannan, entered the Ratisbon Monastery in 1682. [SIG#293]

BRUCE, JEAN, Parish of Bellie, 1710. [NAS.CH1.2.29.3/211]

BRUCE, Dr, a priest in Banffshire, 1710.[NAS.CH1.2.30/1/5]

BUCHAN, EDWARD, gardener to the laird of Garleton, with his wife Bessie Henderson, son John and daughter Barbara, in East Lothian, 1703. [NAS.CH1.2.5.1]

BUCHAN, JAMES, the elder of Auchmacoy, Aberdeen, 1704/1705. [NAS.CH1.2.5.2/155]

BUCHAN, ..., a priest in Aberdeen, 1714. [NLS.ms976.143]

BURDON, HENRY, late Episcopal preacher, in Edinburgh, an apostate and 'a papist' residing near Kennedy's Close, Old Kirk parish, Edinburgh, 1703/1704/1705. [NAS.CH1.2.5.2.149/151; 175/1]

BURGIE, JANET, CUIE, AGNES, a servant in Upper Achinroth, in the parish of Bellie, 1710. [NAS.CH1.2.29.3/211]

BURNE, HELEN, spouse to Thomas Henry late sergeant, 'a papist' in Hamilton's land, Canongait, Edinburgh, 1703/1704/1705. [NAS.CH1.2.5.2.149/151/170]

BURNETT, ALEXANDER, son of the minister of Rayne, a student at the Scots College in Madrid, 1699, and at the Scots College at Douai, 1699. [RSC.I.65/199]

BURNET, MARGARET, born 15 June 1688, daughter of Alexander Burnet a cooper wright, then a Catholic, and his wife Margaret Craw, a Protestant, was baptised on 18 June 1688 by Father Robert Francis in Aberdeen, godfather was Richard Irvine, and the godmother was Margaret Aedie. [SNQ.VIII.180]

BUTTER, ..., of Gormoch, Errol, Perthshire, 1704. [NAS.CH1.2.5.3.203]

BUY, DUNCAN, with his family of three, in the Kirkton of Comer, Kiltarlity, Inverness-shire, 1710. [NAS.CH1.2.29.3]

BUYN, MARGARET, in Ruthven, Strathbogie,1710. [NAS.CH1.2.29.3/209]

BYARS, JOHN, of Coats, 'a papist', in Potter Row, Edinburgh, 1681. [RPCS.VII.729]

BYARS, MARY, sister to the laird of Coats, 'a papist' in Tron Kirk parish, Edinburgh, 1703/1705. [NAS.CH1.2.5.2.151/175/1]

BYRES, GEORGE, a printer in Edinburgh, 'a papist' in Niddrie's Wynd, Tron Kirk parish, Edinburgh, 1703/1704/1705. All his family being Protestants. [NAS.CH1.2.5.2.149/151;175/1]

BYRES, HELEN, aged about 10, 'a papist' in Canongait parish, Edinburgh, 1705. [NAS.CH1.2.5.2.170]

BYRES, JAMES, of Colts, and his sister Mary Byres, 'papists' in Tron Kirk parish, Edinburgh, 1704. [NAS.CH1.2.5.2/149]

BYRES, Mrs MARY, 'a papist' in Canongait, Edinburgh, 1705. [NAS.CH1.2.5.2.170]

CAIRD, ELIZABETH, a servant in Carruchen, Traquair, Dumfries-shire, 1703. [NAS.CH1.2.5.1]

CAIRD, JOHN, servant to Robert Aitkin in Kirkconnel, New Abbey, Dumfries-shire, 1703. [NAS.CH1.2.5.1]

CAIRD, MARION, a tenant or cottar in the town of Cargan, Traquair, Dumfries-shire, 1703. [NAS.CH1.2.5.1]

CAIRD, NICOLAS, in Mabie, Traquair, Dumfries-shire, 1703. [NAS.CH1.2.5.1]

CAIRD, THOMAS, in Carruchen, Traquair, Dumfries-shire, with his wife Janet Pain and children James, and Janet, 1703. [NAS.CH1.2.5.1]

CAIRD, WILLIAM, in Mabie, in Traquair, Dumfries-shire, 1703. [NAS.CH1.2.5.1]

CAMERON, ALEXANDER, his wife Janet Fraser, and 4 children, in Micras, Tullich, Aberdeenshire, 1718. [NAS.CH1.2.7.271]

CAMERON, ALEXANDER, born 17 September 1701, third son of John Cameron of Lochiel, educated at Douai, a Jesuit at Tournai 1730, probably in Strathglass and Strathfarrar, Inverness-shire by 1741, a suspected Jacobite who was captured in Morar in July 1746, died in London. [IR.XXIV.96]

CAMERON, ALEXANDER, a student at the Scots College at Valladolid, 1780, died 20 September 1833. [RSC.I.208]

CAMPBELL, ALEXANDER, of Ardslignish, an apostate, 1725. [NRAS#771/bundle814]

CAMERON, ALAN, born 26 May 1746, son of John Cameron and Anna Chisholm, a student at Douai, 1753. [RSC.I.89]

CAMERON, ALEXANDER, born 28 July 1747 in Braemar, ordained in Rome 1772, bishop of the Lowland District, 1805 to 1825, died 7 February 1828 in Edinburgh. [CDS]

CAMERON, CHARLES, a student at Douai, 1751. [RSC.I.88]

CAMPBELL, COLIN, of Lochnell, born 1689, educated at the Scots College in Paris, 1716, ordained in Paris 1722, a priest in Moidart and from 1739 Ardnamurchan, killed at Culloden 1746. [IR.XVIII.134][SCP#214][NRAS#771/bundle814]

CAMPBELL, DUNCAN, son of Alexander Campbell of Ardslignish, educated at Scalan, Glenlivet, 1725. [NRAS#771/Bundle814]

CAMPBELL, JOHN, son of Alexander Campbell of Ardslignish, educated at Scalan, Glenlivet, 1725. [NRAS#771/Bundle814]

CAMPBELL, ROBERT, of Silvercraig, aged about 70 years, 'a papist' in Glasgow, 1705. [NAS.CH1.2.5.2.173/2]

CAMPBELL, THOMAS, a beggar, and his spouse Bessie Charles, 'papists' in Canongait, Edinburgh, 1703/1704/1705. [NAS.CH1.2.5.2.149/151/170]

CARD, MARION, in Traquair, Orr, Dumfries-shire, 1705. [NAS.CH1.2.5/156]

CARD, MARION, a servant in Twynholm, Kirkcudbrightshire, 1705.
[NAS.CH1.2.5.2]

CARD, THOMAS, and his spouse Janet Paine, in Troquair, Orr, Dumfries-shire, 1705. [NAS.CH1.2.5/156]

CARD, WILLIAM, and spouse Barbara Hutton, in Troquair, Orr, Dumfries-shire, 1705. [NAS.CH1.2.5/156]

CARLYLE, AGNES, in Terregles, Dumfries-shire, 1705. [NAS.CH1.2.5.2]

CARLYLE, SARAH, in New Abbey, Dumfries-shire, 1703. [NAS.CH1.2.5.1]

CARLYLE, ISOBEL, in Dumfries, 1704. [NAS.CH1.5.2]

CARLYLE, JOHN, his wife Marion Wright, and children Robert, William, Mary, Janet and Agnes, in Mabie, Troquair, Orr, Dumfries-shire, 1703/1705. [NAS.CH1.2.5/156]

CARLYLE, MARY, spouse to James Laury, in Troquair, Orr, Dumfries-shire, 1705. [NAS.CH1.2.5/156]

CARLYLE, SARAH, a widow in Dumfries, 1705. [NAS.CH1.2.5.1]

CARLYLE, THOMAS, his spouse Isobel Paine, and children – John, Janet, Isabel and Elizabeth, in Troquair, Orr, Dumfries-shire, 1705. [NAS.CH1.2.5/156]

CARLYLE, WILLIAM, and spouse Janet Wright, in Troquair, Orr, Dumfries-shire, 1705. [NAS.CH1.2.5/156]

CARMICHAEL, BARBARA, servant to James Clerk of Wrightshouses, a 'papist, in West Kirk parish, Edinburgh, 1704. [NAS.CH1.2.5.2.149]

CARMICHAEL, JAMES, at the Ratisbon Seminary in 1756. [SIG#295][RSC.I.253]

CARMICHAEL, JOHN, at the Ratisbon Seminary in 1756. [SIG#295][RSC.I.253]

CARMICHAEL, MARGARET, and her daughter Mary Marr, in Terregles and Kirkgunzeon, Dumfries-shire, 1705. [NAS.CH1.2.5.2]

CARMICHAEL, THOMAS, at the Ratisbon Seminary in 1802. [SIG#295][RSC.I.254]

CARNEGIE, Lord CHARLES, eldest son of the Earl of Southesk. 1673. [RPCS.IV.122]

CARNEGY, JAMES, born 1668, son of William Carnegy a writer in Edinburgh, a student at the Scots College at Douai, 1688, died 173... [RSC.I.60]

CARNFIELDS, Lady, in Aberdeenshire, 1714. [NLS.ms976.143]

CARRON, JAMES, late skipper in Leith, 'apostatised about ten years ago, went to France about two and a half years ago and never returned since', has three children – Margaret Carron aged ten, Jean Carron aged eight, and John Carron aged four years - residing at the head of Rotten Row with Isobel Wilson the mother's sister, who is Protestant', South Leith, 1704. [NAS.CH1.2.5.2.149]

CARRUTHERS, ANDREW, of the Catholic Mission in Munshes, 1798-1813. [NRAS.3666/37/2]

CARRUTHERS, JAMES, his wife Janet Crichton, and sons James and John, in Mabie, Troquair, Orr, Dumfries-shire, 1703,1705. [NAS.CH1.2.5/156]

CARRUTHERS, THOMAS, his spouse Janet Crow, son George, and daughter Mary, in Troquair, Orr, Dumfries-shire, 1705. [NAS.CH1.2.5/156]

CATTENACH, ALEXANDER, in Achintoul, Tullich, Aberdeenshire, 1714, 1718. [NLS.ms976.143][NAS.CH1.2.7.271]

CATTENACH, ARCHIBALD, his wife, and son John, in Tomnafiagh, Glengarden, Aberdeenshire, 1718. [NAS.CH1.2.47.271]

CATTENACH, DONALD, in Achintoul, Tullich, Aberdeenshire, 1718. [NAS.CH1.2.7.271]

CATTENACH, GEORGE, in Fochabers, Morayshire, 1705. [NAS.CH1.2.5/2]

CATTENACH, GEORGE, a servant in Coldham, Parish of Bellie, 1710. [NAS.CH1.2.29.3/211]

CATTENACH, GEORGE, in Glencat,with his wife Elizabeth Duguid, and six young children, and his mother, in Aboyne or Glentanar, 1710. [NAS.CH1.2.29.3]

CATTENACH, JAMES, in Ricarcary, Glengarden, Aberdeenshire, 1718. [NAS.CH1.2.47.271]

CATTENACH, JAMES, from Galloway, educated at the Scots College in Paris 1777, ordained in Paris 1788, a priest in the Highlands from 1788, died in Campbeltown on 3 December 1836. [IR.XVIII.161][SCP#219]

CATTENACH, JOHN, and his wife, in Achintoul, Tullich, Aberdeenshire, 1718. [NAS.CH1.2.7.271]

CATTENACH, JOHN, the younger, and his wife ... Fleming, in Achintoul, Tullich, Aberdeenshire, 1718. [NAS.CH1.2.7.271]

CATTENACH, JOHN, with his wife Isobel Roy and two children, in Forme (?),in Glenmuick, Tullich, and Glengarden, Aberdeenshire, 1718. [NAS.CH1.2.47/284]

CATTENACH, MARGARET, in Fochabers, Morayshire, 1705. [NAS.CH1.2.5/2]

CATTENACH, MARJORIE, Strathaven, Banffshire, 1708. [NAS.CH1.2.30/1/28]

CATTENACH, WILLIAM, in Inveringie, Ardach, with his wife Beatrix Durard, in Glenmuick, Tullich, and Glengarden, Aberdeenshire, 1718. [NAS.CH1.2.47/284]

CHALMERS, ALEXANDER, from Edinburgh, MA Edinburgh University, 1676, a medical student at Rheims, 1681, testament, 1714, Comm. Edinburgh. [RCPE]

CHAMBER, JEAN, widow of John Jamieson a Protestant merchant burgess of Aberdeen, was baptised by Father Robert Francis in Aberdeen on 18 January 1698. [SNQ.VIII.182]

CHANCELLOR, JOHN, late bailie, and his daughter Martha Chancellor aged 14 years, apostates, 'suspected papists' in College Kirk parish, Edinburgh, 1703/1704/1705. "his nearest Protestant relation is Chancellor of Shielhill". [NAS.CH1.2.5.2.149;151;175/1]

CHAPMAN, AGNES, wife to James Reid in Cowie Muir, in the parish of Bellie, 1710. [NAS.CH1.2.29.3/211]

CHARLES, ALEXANDER, born in Edinburgh 1730, son of a painter, at the Ratisbon Seminary, 1739. [RSC.I.252]

CHARLES, ISOBEL, at Sandston, Dunbennan parish, 1710. [NAS.CH1.2.29.3/210]

CHARLES, MARGARET, a servant in Ruthven, Strathbogie,1710. [NAS.CH1.2.29.3/209]

CHEYN, ALEXANDER, schoolmaster at Huntly, Aberdeenshire, 1720. [NLS.ms68.31-32]

CHEYNE, GREGORY, born in Mar around 1672, matriculated at Wurzburg in 1695, ordained in 1697, died 1731. [SF#272/281]

CHEYN, ..., a servant in Liberton, Edinburgh, 1703. [NAS.CH1.2.5.2/151]

CHINIE, JOHN, in Liberton, Edinburgh, 1704. [NAS.CH1.2.5.154]

CHISHOLM, AENEAS, of the Knockfin family, Strathglass, educated at Valladolid in 1774, later a vicar apostolic of the Highland District, and bishop of the Highland District, died on Lismore, 31 July 1818. [IR.XXIV.101][CDS]

CHISHOLM, ALAN, born 1638 in Tweedale, educated at Wurzburg, died in 1703. [SF#272/280]

CHISHOLM, ALEXANDER, and family, in Guisachan, Kiltarlity, Inverness-shire, 1710. [NAS.CH1.2.29.3]

CHISHOLM, ANGUS, born 1749, a student at the Scots College at Valladolid, 1774, later in Lismore, died 28 July 1818. [RSC.I.206]

CHISHOLM, COLIN, brother of John Chisholm of Knockfurn, Inverness-shire, 1703. [NAS.CH1.2.5.2]

CHISHOLM, COLLIN, and family of six or seven, in Guisachan, Kiltarlity, Inverness-shire, 1710. [NAS.CH1.2.29.3]

CHISHOLM, DUNCAN, of Craskie, born 1753, died 25 January 1831, husband of Margaret Bain, born 1756, died 24 February 1848. [Clachan Comair Monumental Inscription, Kerrow, Inverness-shire]

CHISHOLM, JANET, gentlewoman to the Lady Niddrie, an apostate and a 'papist', 1704. [NAS.CH1.2.5.2.149]

CHISHOLM, JOHN, of Knockfurn, 1703. [NAS.CH1.2.5.2]

CHISHOLM, JOHN, son of Valentine Chisholm and Janet MacDonal,born in Strathglass, Inverness-shire, during 1753, educated at Dinant in 1766, ordained at Douai in 1777, a priest in Strathglass, died in Lismore on 8 July 1812. [IR.XVIII.154][RSC.I.93]

CHISHOLM, JOHN, of Knockline, born 2 January 1762, died 26 January 1810, husband of Jean Fraser, third daughter of William Fraser of Culbokie, born 11 April 1766, died 6 June 1799, parents of John and others. [Clachan Comair Monumental Inscription, Kerrow, Inverness-shire]

CHISHOLM, THOMAS, the younger, in Kilmorack, 1673. [IR.XXIV.80]

CHISHOLM, WILLIAM, and family of eight, in Kirkton of Comar, Kiltarlity, Inverness-shire, 1710. [NAS.CH1.2.29.3]

CHRISTIE, JANET, a subtenant in Cumry, in Ruthven, Strathbogie,1710. [NAS.CH1.2.29.3/209]

CHRISTIE, JOHN, a subtenant in Comry, in Ruthven, Strathbogie,1710. [NAS.CH1.2.29.3/209]

CHRISTIE, KATHERINE, in Baladan, Glengarden, Aberdeenshire, 1718. [NAS.CH1.2.47.271]

CLAPERTON, THOMAS, in Fochabers, Morayshire, 1720. [NLS.ms68.31-32]

CLARKE, ANDREW, rector of the Scots College in Madrid, 1727. [RSC.I.203]

CLELAND, GRISSELL, relict of James Hepburn an armorer, 'a papist' in Canongait, Edinburgh, 1704/1705. [NAS.CH1.2.5.2.149/170]

CLERK, EDWARD, servant to the Earl of Nithsdale, in Terregles, Dumfries-shire, 1703. [NAS.CH1.2.5.1]

CLERK, ELSPETH, in College Kirk parish, Edinburgh, 1703. [NAS.CH1.2.5.2/151]

CLERK, GEORGE, a child in Wrightshouses, West Kirk parish, Edinburgh, 1704. [NAS.CH1.2.5.154]

CLERK, HELEN, in Fochabers, Morayshire, 1705. [NAS.CH1.2.5/2]

CLERK, JAMES, of Wrightshouses, and his spouse Mary Richard, and children George, Elizabeth, Margaret, and Mary, apostate 'papists' in Peebles Wynd, Tron Kirk parish, Edinburgh, 1704/1705. A son, named Francis, lives in London, while another, named Robert, is at school in Strathbogie. Sir John Clerk of Penicuik is the nearest Protestant relation. [NAS.CH1.2.5.2.149; 175/1]

CLERK, JAMES, at the Waulkmiln of Milton, parish of Keith, Banffshire, with Margaret Forbes from Enzie, apostates, 1710. [NAS.CH1.2.30/1/5]

CLERK, JANET, in Dalbeattie, Orr, Dumfries-shire,1705. [NAS.CH1.2.5/156]

CLERK, or KEY, JOHN, and his family of six, Kiltarlity, Inverness-shire, 1710. [NAS.CH1.2.29.3]

CLERK, MARY, a child in Wrightshouses, West Kirk parish, Edinburgh, 1704. [NAS.CH1.2.5.154]

CLERK, REBECCA or ROBERTA, a 'papist', spouse to James Wright, a cook, a Protestant in College Kirk parish, Edinburgh, 1703/1704/1705. [NAS.CH1.2.5.2.149; 151;175/1]

CLERK, THOMAS, was born on 27 April 1696, son of James Clerk, a Protestant, and his wife Christian Robertson, a Catholic, was baptised on 1 October 1696 by Father Robert Francis. [SNQ.VIII.182]

CLERK, WILLIAM, born 1668, son of William Clerk and Joanna Cars in Edinburgh, a student at the Scots College at Douai, 1688. [RSC.I.60]

CLERK, WILLIAM, and his wife Isobel Bremner, at the Raws of Huntly, Dunbennan parish, 1710. [NAS.CH1.2.29.3/210]

CLOVA, Lady, in Angus, 1704. [NAS.CH1.2.5/204]

CLURE, JANET, in Colvend, Dumfries-shire, 1704. [NAS.CH1.2.5.2]

COATS, or COLTS, Lady, in Edinburgh, 'a papist' in Tron Kirk parish, Edinburgh, 1704/1705. [NAS.CH1.2.5.2.149; 175/1]

COBBAN, JOHN, and his wife Janet Duncan, in Balnaboth, Glass, 1710. [NAS.CH1.2.29.3]

COBBAN, WILLIAM, a piper in Fochabers, with Jean Coban, Morayshire, 1705, 1710. [NAS.CH1.2.5/2; 2.29.3/210]

COLINSON, F., from Aberdeen, at the Monastery of Ratisbon from 1687, died 1686. [SIG#293]

COLLIE, ELIZABETH, daughter of George Collie, a Protestant, and his wife Jean Thomson, a Catholic, in the parish of St Machar, Old Aberdeen, was baptised as a Protestant as an infant, later baptised on 29 September 1696 by Father Robert Francis. [SNQ.VIII.181]

COLLIE, JANET, daughter of Thomas Collie, sheriff's officer, and his wife Rathvin Thomson, in the parish of St Machar, Old Aberdeen, was baptised as a Protestant as an infant, later baptised on 29 September 1697 by Father Robert Francis. [SNQ.VIII.182]

COLLISON, GEORGE, born 1678, son of Robert Collison and Margaret Duguid in Aberdeen, a student at the Scots College at Douai, 1693. [RSC.I.62]

COLLISTON, JEAN, a servant at Traquair, Peebles-shire, 1705. [NAS.CH1.2.5.3/176]

COMISTON, Lady, in Edinburgh, 'a papist' in Old Kirk parish, Edinburgh, 1705. [NAS.CH1.2.5.2.175/1]

COOK, ANDREW, from the Diocese of Aberdeen, at the Ratisbon Monastery from 1671, died 1721. [SIG#293]

COOK, CATHERINE, born 1760, daughter of John Cook, tenant in Campsy, Stobhall. [NAS.CC8.6.36]

COOK, GEORGE, an improver on the Muir of Deskford, 1772. [NAS.GD248.3405.8]

COOK, JOHN, a weaver in Campsie, Cargill, Perthshire, and his wife Margaret Miller, and children, 1704. [NAS.CH1.2.5.3.203]

COPELAND, GEORGE, and his wife Janet Ramsay, in Dalbeattie, Orr, Dumfries-shire, 1705. [NAS.CH1.2.5/156]

CORSBIE, JAMES, a cottar in Munches, with his wife Isobel Chrystie, and children Andrew and James, in Buittle, Kirkcudbrightshire, 1705. [NAS.CH1.2.5.2]

CORSON, JANET, spouse of John Allan tenant in Townhead of Kirkconnel, and their children – John aged 12, Elizabeth aged 11, Esther aged 9, and William aged 3, New Abbey, Dumfries-shire, 1703. [NAS.CH1.2.5.1]

CORSON, HELEN, aged 25, sister of Robert Corson, in New Abbey, Dumfries-shire, 1703. [NAS.CH1.2.5.1]

CORSON, JOHN, tenant in Lochhill, daughters Agnes aged 12, Elizabeth aged 18, and Rachel, New Abbey, Dumfries-shire, 1703. [NAS.CH1.2.5.1]

CORSON, MARGARET, aged 3, in New Abbey, Dumfries-shire, 1703. [NAS.CH1.2.5.1]

CORSON, MARION, aged 12, in New Abbey, Dumfries-shire, 1703. [NAS.CH1.2.5.1]

CORSON, ROBERT, a tenant in Kirkconnel, daughter Agnes aged 2, son James aged 4, John aged 6, in New Abbey, Dumfries-shire, 1703. [NAS.CH1.2.5.1]

COUPAR, ALEXANDER, a cobbler in Aberdeen, 1704/1705. [NAS.CH1.2.5.2/155]

COUPAR, ALEXANDER, in Aboyne or Glentanar, 1710. [NAS.CH1.2.29.3]

COUPAR, JAMES, his wife Janet Smith, in Glengarden, Aberdeenshire, 1718. [NAS.CH1.2.47.271]

COUPAR, JANET, and her daughter Margaret Naughty, in Brunston, Kinnoir parish, 1710. [NAS.CH1.2.29.3/210]

COUPAR, MARJORIE, born 13 March 1689, daughter of Alexander Coupar a cordiner in Aberdeen, was baptised by Father Robert Francis on 14 March 1689. [SNQ.VIII.181]

COUPLAND, GEORGE, a cottar in Munches, with Mary Wyllie his spouse, and children Janet, William, James, and Barbara, in Buittle, Kirkcudbrightshire, 1705. [NAS.CH1.2.5.2]

COUPLAND, NICOLA, spouse of George McK.... a cottar in Buittle, Kirkcudbrightshire, 1705. [NAS.CH1.2.5.2]

COUPLAND, THOMAS, a cottar in Buittle, and his wife Sarah Wilson, in Kirkcudbrightshire, 1705. [NAS.CH1.2.5.2]

COUPLAND, THOMAS, a cottar in Munches, with his wife Agnes Thomson, and children William, Margaret, and Thomas, in Buittle, Kirkcudbrightshire, 1705. [NAS.CH1.2.5.2]

COUTTS, ELISABETH, wife of John Doue, in Micras, Tullich, Aberdeenshire, 1718. [NAS.CH1.2.7.271]

COUTTS, JOHN, and his wife, in Rianeffen, Tullich, Aberdeenshire, 1718. [NAS.CH1.2.7.271]

COUTS, MARGARET, wife of Robert Irvine laird of Cults, was baptised by Father Robert Francis in Aberdeen on 18 January 1698. [SNQ.VIII.182]

COUTTS, THOMAS, in Riahloin, 1718. [NAS.CH1.2.7.271]

COUTTS, WILLIAM, a student at Douai, 1742. [RSC.I.85]

COWIE, ALEXANDER, tacksman of the Petty Customs of Banff, 1794. [NAS.SC2.72.4]

COWIE, JAMES, a farmer in Auchinhive, Banffshire, 1794. [NAS.SC2.72.4]

CRANSTON, JEAN, married Sir Alexander Livingstone of Westquarter, on 28 November 1782. [IR.XVII.50]

CREICHTON, THOMAS, chamberlain to Lord Drummond, and his wife Beatrix Drummond and eight children, in Cargill, Perthshire, 1704.[NAS.CH1.2.5.3.203]

CRICHTON, LOUIS, 'a declared and bigoted papist', 1680. [RPCS.VI.414]

CRICHTON, PLACID, of Auchengoul, at the Monastery of Wurzburg in 1689, died 1730. [SF#281]

CRIGHTON, GEORGE, at the Ratisbon Seminary in 1719. [SIG#294]

CRIGHTON, GEORGE, born 25 September 1725, at the Ratisbon Seminary, 1735. [RSC.I.251]

CRIGHTON, GREGOR, of Auchengoul in the Diocese of Aberdeen, at the Ratisbon Monastery from 1684, died 1748. [SIG#293]

CROCKET, AGNES, spouse to John Ridge the elder, in Kirkconnel, Dumfries-shire, 1703. [NAS.CH1.2.5.1]

CROCKET, ISOBEL, a cottar or tenant in the town of Cargan, and her daughter Isobel Crocket, Troquair, Orr, Dumfries-shire,1705. [NAS.CH1.2.5/156]

CROCKET, MARGARET, spouse to John Ferguson, and son John Ferguson, in Carruchen, Troquair, Orr, Dumfries-shire, 1705. [NAS.CH1.2.5/156]

CROCKET, NICOLAS, tenant in Townhead of Kirkconnel, Dumfries-shire, 1703. [NAS.CH1.2.5.1]

CRON, JAMES, with his wife Janet Carlyle, in Troquair, Orr, Dumfries-shire, 1705. [NAS.CH1.2.5/156]

CROOKSHANK, ALEXANDER, rector of the Scots College at Douai, 1748. [RSC.I.86]

CROOKSHANK, WILLIAM, in Gaularick, and his wife Isobel Stuart, Strathaven, Banffshire, 1708. [NAS.CH1.2.30/1/28]

CROW, MARGARET, Lady Lumsden,in Edinburgh, 'a papist' residing in Liberton's Wynd, New North Kirk parish, Edinburgh, 1704/ 1705. [NAS.CH1.2.5.2.149; 175/1]

CRUICKSHANK, ALEXANDER, with his wife Margaret Crabb, and sons John and George, in Hillend, in Ruthven, Strathbogie,1710. [NAS.CH1.2.29.3/209]

CRUICKSHANK, ANN, in the parish of St Machar, Aberdeen, was baptised as a Protestant when an infant, baptised by Father Robert Francis on 29 September 1696. [SNQ.VIII.181]

CRUICKSHANK, GEORGE, in Gibstoun, Ruthven, Strathbogie,1710. [NAS.CH1.2.29.3/209]

CRUICKSHANK, GEORGE, with his wife Anna Stuart, in Robestoun, Kinnoir parish, 1710. [NAS.CH1.2.29.3/210]

CRUICKSHANK, JAMES, a weaver in Aberdeen, 1704/1705. [NAS.CH1.2.5.2/155]

CRUICKSHANK, JAMES, tenant in Chapelford, with his wife Agnes Mitchel, and younger daughter Agnes, parish of Bellie, 1710. [NAS.CH1.2.29.3]

CRUICKSHANK, JAMES, at the Ratisbon Seminary in 1800. [SIG#295]

CRUICKSHANK, JANET, and her daughter Janet Leith, in Ruthven, Strathbogie, 1710. [NAS.CH1.2.29.3/209]

CRUICKSHANK, JANET, at the Raws of Huntly, Dunbennan parish, 1710. [NAS.CH1.2.29.3/210]

CRUICKSHANK, JOHN, born 14 April 1693, son of Robert Cruickshank, a Catholic, and Elspet Gray, a Protestant, in the parish of Ruthven, was baptised there by Father Robert Francis on 15 April 1693. [SNQ.VIII.181]

CRUICKSHANK, JOHN, and his wife Helen Hay, in Robestoun, Kinnoir parish, 1710. [NAS.CH1.2.29.3/210]

CRUICKSHANK, JOHN, a servant in Cowie Muir, in the parish of Bellie, 1710. [NAS.CH1.2.29.3/211]

CRUICKSHANK, JOHN, MD, at the Ratisbon Seminary in 1713. [SIG#294][RSC.I.249]

CRUICKSHANK, MARGARET, in Ruthven, Strathbogie,1710. [NAS.CH1.2.29.3/209]

CRUICKSHANK, MARGARET, in Cumry, in Ruthven, Strathbogie,1710. [NAS.CH1.2.29.3/209]

CRUICKSHANK, ROBERT, a subtenant in Cormollet, Ruthven, Strathbogie,1710. [NAS.CH1.2.29.3/209]

CRUICKSHANK, WILLIAM, a weaver in Aberdeen, 1704/1705. [NAS.CH1.2.5.2/155]

CRUICKSHANK, WILLIAM, in Ruthven, Strathbogie,1710. [NAS.CH1.2.29.3/209]

CRUICKSHANK, WILLIAM, tenant in Cowie Muir, with his wife Margaret Robertson, and son James, in the parish of Bellie, 1710. [NAS.CH1.2.29.3/211]

CUIE, AGNES, a servant in Upper Achinroth, in the parish of Bellie, 1710. [NAS.CH1.2.29.3/211]

CUIE, ALEXANDER, a smith, and his wife Helen Hay, Parish of Bellie, 1710. [NAS.CH1.2.29.3/211]

CUIE, JAMES, a smith in Fochabers, Morayshire, 1705; and his wife Christian Godsman, also his mother Marjory Gilbert, 1710. [NAS.CH1.2.5/2; 2.29.3/210]

CUIE, JAMES, a smith, his wife Marjorie Gilbert, and children James, Alexander and Isabel, in Fochabers, Morayshire, 1705. [NAS.CH1.2.5/2, 187]

CUIE, JAMES, a tenant, with his wife Agnes Geddes, and children William and Annie, in Tullo, Parish of Bellie, 1710. [NAS.CH1.2.29.3/211]

CUIE, JOHN, servant to Boynd, parish of Bellie, 1710. [NAS.CH1.2.29.3]

CUIE, MARGARET, in Cottonhill, Parish of Bellie, 1710. [NAS.CH1.2.29.3/211]

CUIE, WILLIAM, a tenant in Cowie Muir, with his wife Margaret Reid, and children Elspet and Alexander, in the parish of Bellie, 1710. [NAS.CH1.2.29.3/211]

CUMINE, BEATRIX, 'excommunicated for habitual uncleanliness and apostacy', in Ardach, in Glenmuick, Tullich, and Glengarden, Aberdeenshire,1718. [NAS.CH1.2.47/284]

CUMMING, ALEXANDER, son of ..... Cumming of Alathan and Anna Leslie, a student at Douai, 1742. [RSC.I.85]

CURRIE, ..., a priest in the Outer Hebrides, 1720. [NLS.ms68.31-32]

CUSHNIE, ANDREW, servant to the laird of Drum, baptised as a Protestant when young, baptised as a Catholic in the parish of Dalmaik by Father Robert Francis on 29 March 1698. [SNQ.VIII.182]

CUTHBERT, ..., born 1736, son of George Cuthbert of Castlehill, Inverness, and Mary Mackintosh, educated at the Scots College in Paris 1747, ordained in France 1762, Bishop of Rodez, 1781, died in London 14 January 1813. [SCP#217]

DALGLEISH, GEORGE, born 1681, son of Colin Douglas and Elizabeth Irvine in the diocese of Ross, educated at the Scots College in Paris, ordained at Scothouse in 1707, died in Morar on 29 April 1731. [SCP#212]

DALZELL, JAMES, son of Colonel John Dalzell brother of the Earl of Carnwath, a student at the Scots College in Madrid, 1734. [RSC.I.200]

DANNIE, JAMES, a weaver in Canitouichal, Glengarden, Aberdeenshire,1718. [NAS.CH1.2.47.271]

DARNELL, JOHN, in Robestoun, Kinnoir parish, 1710. [NAS.CH1.2.29.3/210]

DASON, ANDREW, in Ruthven, Strathbogie,1710. [NAS.CH1.2.29.3/209]

DASON, ISOBEL, at Stonehouse, Kinnore parish, 1710. [NAS.CH1.2.29.3/210]

DASON, JAMES, in Earnhill, Ruthven, Strathbogie,1710. [NAS.CH1.2.29.3/209]

DASON, JAMES, in Ruthven, Strathbogie,1710. [NAS.CH1.2.29.3/209]

DASON, JAMES, in the Muir of Kinnore parish, 1710. [NAS.CH1.2.29.3/210]

DASON, JEAN, in Achinboe, Kinnore parish, 1710. [NAS.CH1.2.29.3/210]

DASON, JOHN, and his daughter Margaret, in Lomond, Kinnore parish, 1710. [NAS.CH1.2.29.3/210]

DASON, JOHN, a servant in Cross, Kinnore parish, 1710. [NAS.CH1.2.29.3/210]

DASON, MARGARET, in Ruthven, Strathbogie,1710. [NAS.CH1.2.29.3/209]

DASON, WILLIAM, in Ruthven, Strathbogie,1710. [NAS.CH1.2.29.3/209]

DAUBIE, ISABEL, servant to the Earl of Nithsdale, in Terregles, Dumfries-shire, 1703. [NAS.CH1.2.5.1]

DAVIDSON, CLAUD, a servant at Traquair, Peebles-shire, 1705. [NAS.CH1.2.5.3/176]

DAVIDSON, ELSPET, in Killochill, Dalbeattie, Orr, Dumfries-shire, 1705. [NAS.CH1.2.5/156]

DAVIDSON, HELEN, in Dalbeattie, Orr, Dumfries-shire, 1705. [NAS.CH1.2.5/156]

DAVIDSON, ISOBEL, spouse to John Nicolson, at Schoolgreen and Milnton, the Raws of Huntly, Dunbennan parish, 1710. [NAS.CH1.2.29.3/210]

DAVIDSON, JAMES, in Carlogie, Aboyne or Glentanar, Aberdeenshire, 1704. [NAS.CH1.2.5/190]

DAVIDSON, JANET, in Buittle, Kirkcudbrightshire, 1705. [NAS.CH1.2.5.2]

DAVIDSON, JEAN, servant to the Earl of Nithsdale, in Terregles, Dumfries-shire, 1703. [NAS.CH1.2.5.1]

DAVIDSON, JEAN, widow of John Fordyce of Achincrive, and her daughterElizabeth Fordyce, formerly in Chapel of Garich, then in Rothiemay, Strathbogie, 1710. [NAS.CH1.2.29.3]

DAVIDSON, JOHN, the elder, his wife Janet Kier, and children John and Elizabeth, in Tullich, Glengarden, Aberdeenshire, 1718. [NAS.CH1.2.47.271]

DAVIDSON, JOHN, a student at the Scots College at Valladolid, 1780, died in Greenock on 8 January 1815. [RSC.I.208]

DAVIDSON, MARY, in Dalbeattie, Orr, Dumfries-shire,1705. [NAS.CH1.2.5/156]

DAVIDSON, WILLIAM, of Balnacraig, his spouse Margaret Gordon, and children Alexander, Elizabeth, Norman, William, Hew, Ann, Margaret, and Janet, in Aboyne or Glentanar, Aberdeenshire, 1704. [NAS.CH1.2.5/187]

DAVIDSON, WILLIAM, a farmer in Kempcairn, Banffshire, 1794. [NAS.SC2.72.4]

DAVISON, MARY, a servant in College Kirk parish, Edinburgh, 1703. [NAS.CH1.2.5.2/151]

DAWSON, ANDREW, a student at the Scots College at Valladolid, 1777, DIED IN Huntly on 4 September 1788. [RSC.I.207]

DEASON, JOHN, born 1774 in Huntly, Aberdeenshire, at Ratisbon Seminary from 1788, ordained on 1797, died 21 November 1855. [RSC.I.254]

DECANTO, JAMES, a musician in Edinburgh, and his spouse Beatrix Baillie, 'a papist' in Blackfriars Wynd, Tron Kirk parish, Edinburgh, 1703/1704/ 1705. [NAS.CH1.2.5.2.149/151; 175/1]

DESON, GEORGE, a weaver in Banff, Banffshire, 1794. [NAS.SC2.72.4]

DESON, JAMES, a weaver in Macduff, Banffshire, 1794. [NAS.SC2.72.4]

DEWAR, ANNA, in Auchterarder, Perthshire, 1703. [NAS.CH1.2.5.2]

DICKSON, AGNES, in Green Milne, Caerlaverock, Dumfries-shire, 1705. [NAS.CH1.2.5.1]

DICKSON, AGNES, wife of Homer Jamieson, an apostate, in Caerlaverock, Dumfries-shire, 1704. [NAS.CH1.2.5.2]

DINNIE, FRANCIS, a tenant in Aboyne or Glentanar, Aberdeenshire, 1704. [NAS.CH1.2.5/190]

DIXON, MARIE, in Fochabers, Morayshire, 1705. [NAS.CH1.2.5/2]

DIXON, Mrs, a schoolmistress in Fochabers, Morayshire, 1705. [NAS.CH1.2.5/187]

DOBIE, ISABEL, in Terregles parish, Dumfries-shire,1705. [NAS.CH1.2.5.2]

DOBIE, JEAN, in Terregles and Kirkgunzeon parish, Dumfries-shire, 1705. [NAS.CH1.2.5.2]

DONALD, JEAN, in Fochabers, Morayshire, 1705. [NAS.CH1.2.5/2]

DONALD, MARGARET, in Fochabers, Morayshire, 1705. [NAS.CH1.2.5/2]

DONALD, MARGARET, in Ruthven, Strathbogie,1710. [NAS.CH1.2.29.3/209]

DONALD, JANET, in Ruthven, Strathbogie,1710. [NAS.CH1.2.29.3/209]

DONALD, JANET, in Bogtoun, Kinnoir parish, 1710. [NAS.CH1.2.29.3/210]

DONALD, JEAN, in Fochabers, 1710. [NAS.CH1.2.29.3/210]

DONALDSON, JAMES, a missionary at Preshome, 1699. [IR.XXIV.85]

DONALDSON, JANET, in Terregles and Kirkgunzeon, Dumfries-shire, 1705. [NAS.CH1.2.5.2]

DONALDSON, REBEKAH, in Fochabers, 1710. [NAS.CH1.2.29.3/210]

DONALDSON, Mr, a priest in Banffshire, 1710, in Aberdeen, 1714. [NAS.CH1.2.30/1/5] [NLS.ms976.143]

DOUGLAS, Dame ANNA, Lady Comeston, daughter of Lord Mordington, and her children Walter and Jean Potterfield, in Collinton, Edinburgh, 1703. [NAS.CH1.2.5.2/151]

DOUGLAS, ELIZABETH, spouse to John Campbell a soldier in the Town Guard, in Veitch's land, Canongait, Edinburgh, 1704, 1705. [NAS.CH1.2.5.2/149, 154]

DOUGLAS, HELEN, a servant in Garleton, East Lothian, 1703. [NAS.CH1.2.5.1]

DOUGLAS, Mrs HELEN, in Edinburgh. 'a papist' in College Kirk parish, Edinburgh, 1704/1705. [NAS.CH1.2.5.2.149;175/1]

DOUGLAS, JEAN, in College Kirk parish, Edinburgh, 1703. [NAS.CH1.2.5.2/151]

DOUGLAS, WILLIAM, a priest in Bellie, Banffshire, 1710. [NAS.CH1.2.30/1/5]

DOUNIE, PATRICK, servant to James Wauchop, 'a papist' in New Kirk parish, Edinburgh, 1704/1705. [NAS.CH1.2.5.2.149;175/1]

DOWNIE, ANDREW, a cottar in Athelstoneford, East Lothian, his wife Margaret Adamson and three children including Euphan, 1703. [NAS.CH1.2.5.1]

DRUMMOND, ALEXANDER, a priest in Auchterarder, Perthshire, 1703, 1714. [NAS.CH [NLS.ms976.143]

DRUMMOND, ANDREW, son of the Duke of Melfort, a student at the Scots College at Douai, 1694. [RSC.I.62]

DRUMMOND, CHARLES, born 1681, son of the Duke of Perth, a student at the Scots College at Douai, 1693. [RSC.I.62]

DRUMMOND, EDWARD, in Auchterarder, Perthshire, 1703. [NAS.CH1.2.5.2]

DRUMMOND, FRANCIS, born 1672, from Edinburgh, son of George Drummond, a student at the Scots College at Douai, 1688. [RSC.I.59]

DRUMMOND, JAMES, born 1682, son of Ludovic Drummond, educated at the Scots College at Douai 1693, and the Scots College in Paris from 1702 to 1704. [SCP#213][RSC.I.62]

DRUMMOND, JAMES, in Auchterarder, Perthshire, 1703. [NAS.CH1.2.5.2]

DRUMMOND, JOHN, born 1679, son of the Duke of Perth, a student at the Scots College at Douai, 1693. [RSC.I.62]

DRUMMOND, JOHN, the elder of Pitkellenie, Auchterarder, Perthshire, 1703. [NAS.CH1.2.5.2]

DRUMMOND, JOHN, son of Ludovic Drummond, was educated at the Scots College in Paris from 1702 to 1706. [SCP#213]

DRUMMOND, LEWIS, in Auchterarder, Perthshire,1703. [NAS.CH1.2.5.2]

DRUMMOND, LUDOVICK, of Wester Feddalls, Auchterarder, Perthshire, chamberlain to Lord Drummond, 1703. [NAS.CH1.2.5.2]

DRUMMOND, Lady MARY, Countess of Marischal, residing in Fetteresso, Kincardineshire, with daughters Lady Mary Keith, and Lady Anna Keith, 1704. [NAS.CH1.2.5.3/201]

DRUMMOND, PATRICK, late servant in the Tolbooth, 'a papist' in Blackfriars Wynd, Tron Kirk parish, Edinburgh, 1704/1705. [NAS.CH1.2.5.2.149; 175/1]

DRUMMOND, PHILLIP, a student at the Scots College at Douai, 1700. [RSC.I.60]

DRUMMOND, REGINALD, a student at the Scots College at Douai, 1700. [RSC.I.65]

DRUMMOND, THOMAS, son of the Duke of Melfort, a student at the Scots College at Douai, 1692. [RSC.I.61]

DRUMMOND, WILLIAM, born 1686, son of the Duke of Melfort, a student at the Scots College at Douai, 1692. [RSC.I.61]

DRUMMOND, ..., of Eastfield, an advocate in Lady Yester parish, 1703. [NAS.CH1.2.5.2/151]

DRUMMOND, Lord, in Auchterarder, Perthshire, 1703. [NAS.CH1.2.5.2]

DUBOG, JANET, in Forme (?),in Glenmuick, Tullich, and Glengarden, Aberdeenshire,1718. [NAS.CH1.2.47/284]

DUCANTO, ..., a musician and schoolmaster in Tron Kirk parish, Edinburgh, 1703. [NAS.CH1.2.5.2/153]

DUFF, JANET, wife to John Bain Campbell in Salachar, Little Dunkeld, Perthshire, 1704. [NAS.CH1.2.5.3.203]

DUFF, JOHN, a student at the Scots College at Douai, 1686. [RSC.I.59]

DUFF, MARGARET, in Broomhead, spouse to William Boniman there, Glass parish, 1710. [NAS.CH1.2.29.3]

DUFF, ROBERT, in Hillockhead, Botriphnie, 1710. [NAS.CH1.2.29.3]

DUFFUS, GEORGE, a brewer and vintner in Fochabers, Morayshire, with his wife Anna Gordon, and children George, John, and Alexander, 1705; with his children Alexander, George, James, and Mary, in Fochabers, 1710. [NAS.CH1.2.5/2, 187; 2.1.29.3/210]

DUFFUS, JAMES, son of George Duffus in Fochabers, Morayshire, sent abroad for education, 1719. [NLS.ms68.31-32]

DUFFUS, MARGARET, with four children, in Fochabers, Morayshire, 1705. [NAS.CH1.2.5/2]

DUFFUS, MARGARET, a servant in Fochabers, Morayshire, 1705. [NAS.CH1.2.5/187]

DUFFUS, MARGARET, in the Parish of Bellie, 1710. [NAS.CH1.2.29.3/211]

DUGISON, MARY, servant to the Auchmuties in College Kirk parish, Edinburgh, 1703. [NAS.CH1.2.5.2]

DUGUID, CHARLES, a student at Douai, 1756. [RSC.I.90]

DUGUID, HENRY, born 1748, son of Patrick Duguid baron of Auchenhove and Aemilia Irvine, a student at Douai, 1760. [RSC.I.92]

DUGUID, JAMES, son of Patrick Duguid of Auchenhove and Aemilie Irvine, a student at Douai, 1751. [RSC.I.88]

DUGUID, JOHN, at the Ratisbon Seminary in 1764. [SIG#295][RSC.I.253]

DUGUID, PATRICK, a student at Douai, 1765. [RSC.I.92]

DUGUID, ROBERT, of Auchinhive, Lumphannan, Aberdeenshire, and his wife Tresa Leslie, 1710. [NAS.CH1.2.29.3/208]

DUGUID, ROBERT, at the Ratisbon Seminary, 1723. [RSC.I.251]

DUMBRECK, GEORGE, a glover in Fochabers, Morayshire, his wife Janet Dallas, and Janet Dumbreck, Morayshire, 1705; a glover, with Janet Dallas his wife, and their children Jean and Thomas, in Bellie, 1710. [NAS.CH1.2.5/2; CH1.2.29.3]

DUMBRECK, ISOBEL, in Fochabers, 1710. [NAS.CH1.2.29.3/210]

DUMBRECK, MARGARET, in Fochabers, 1710. [NAS.CH1.2.29.3/210]

DUMBRECK, PETER, servant to the Marquess of Huntly, parish of Bellie, 1710. [NAS.CH1.2.29.3]

DUNBAR, ALEXANDER, in Pluscarden, Morayshire, 1705. [NAS.CH1.2.5/2]

DUNBAR, JOHN, from Argyll, at Ratisbon Monastery in 1681. [SIG#293]

DUNBAR, NICOLAS, from Ratisbon Monastery, captured at Feddarate and imprisoned in Canongait Tolbooth in 1691. [RPCS.XVI.529]

DUNBAR, ROBERT, a student at the Scots College at Douai, 1694. [RSC.I.63]

DUNBAR, ROBERT, servant to William Thomson, in Campbell's land, Canongait, Edinburgh, 1704. [NAS.CH1.2.5.2/149]

DUNBAR, Mrs, in Stone Laws Close, Old Kirk parish, Edinburgh, 1703. [NAS.CH1.2.5.2/151]

DUNCAN, AUGUSTUS, at Ratisbon Monastery in 1736. [SIG#294]

DUNCAN, GEORGE, a merchant burgess of Aberdeen, son of George Duncan a Protestant in Maaryculter, was baptised as a Protestant when young, later as a Catholic by Father Robert Francis in Aberdeen on 18 December 1697; 1705, 1714. [SNQ.VIII.182][NAS.CH1.2.5.2] [NLS.ms976.143]

DUNCAN, GEORGE, son of John Duncan and Catherine..... in Edinburgh, educated at the Scots College in Paris 1724, ordained at Scalan, Banffshire, in 1734, Rector of Scalan 1758, died in Edinburgh in 1761. [IR.XVIII.135]

DUNCAN, JOHN, with his wife Mary Gordon, and children, in Echt, Aberdeenshire, 1710. [NAS.CH1.2.29.3]

DUNCAN, JOHN, and his wife Elspet Brown, in Gibstoun, Kinnoir parish, 1710. [NAS.CH1.2.29.3/210]

DUNCAN, JOHN, in Robestoun, Kinnoir parish, 1710. [NAS.CH1.2.29.3/210]

DUNCAN, RICHARD, a glover in Banff, Banffshire, 1794. [NAS.SC2.72.4]

DUNCAN, THOMAS, a gardener in Banff, Banffshire, 1794. [NAS.SC2.72.4]

DUNDASS, ..., a student at the Scots College at Douai, 1686. [RSC.I.59]

DURARD, ALAN, the elder, with his wife Isabel Forbes, with son Calum and another three children, in Ardach, in Glenmuick, Tullich, and Glengarden, Aberdeenshire, 1718. [NAS.CH1.2.47/284]

DURARD, ALAN, the younger, with his wife Isobel Coutts and two children, in Ardach, in Glenmuick, Tullich, and Glengarden, Aberdeenshire, 1718. [NAS.CH1.2.47/284]

DURARD, JOHN, with his wife Isabel Keir, and three children, in Ardach, in Glenmuick, Tullich, and Glengarden, Aberdeenshire, 1718. [NAS.CH1.2.47/284]

DURARD, PATRICK, father of Alan Durard the younger, in Ardach, in Glenmuick, Tullich, and Glengarden, Aberdeenshire, 1718. [NAS.CH1.2.47/284]

DURHAM, ELIZABETH, mother of the laird of Kirkconnel, New Abbey, Dumfries-shire, 1703. [NAS.CH1.2.5.1]

DUTHIE, WILLIAM, son of John Duthie and Mary Henderson in the diocese of Aberdeen, a convert, educated at the Scots College in Paris, ordained in Paris 1737, schoolmaster at Scalan, Banffshire, 1741-1758, later in Paris, a missionary in Strathbogie, Aberdeenshire, died in Huntly on 7 January 1785. [IR.XVII.52][SCP#216]

DYRY, HENRY, a miller in Ruthven, with his wife Jean Lobban, and son James, in Strathbogie,1710. [NAS.CH1.2.29.3/209]

EBBURN or OPPURN, JOANNO, spouse to Edward Reid a hoy-boy in Toderick's Wynd, Edinburgh, 'a papist' in Tron Kirk parish, Edinburgh, 1704/1705. [NAS.CH1.2.5.2.149; 175/1]

EDGAR, ELIZABETH, spouse to William Atcheson, in Liberton, Edinburgh, 1704. [NAS.CH1.2.5.154]

EDGAR, ELSPET, an apostate and a 'papist' in Liberton parish, Edinburgh, 1704. [NAS.CH1.2.5.2.149]

EDGAR, JAMES, and his sons Robert and William, in Troquair, Orr, Dumfries-shire, 1705. [NAS.CH1.2.5/156]

EDGAR, MARGARET, in New Abbey, Dumfries-shire, 1703. [NAS.CH1.2.5.1]

EDWARD, ADAM, servant to the Marquess of Huntly, parish of Bellie, 1710. [NAS.CH1.2.29.3]

EDWARD, BETTIE, servant to the Marquess of Huntly, parish of Bellie, 1710. [NAS.CH1.2.29.3]

EDWARD, ADAM, in Fochabers, Morayshire, 1705. [NAS.CH1.2.5/2]

EDWARD, JOHN, a footman at Gordon Castle, Morayshire, 1705. [NAS.CH1.2.5/187]

EDWARD, MARGARET, in Charleston, Aboyne or Glentanar, Aberdeenshire, 1704. [NAS.CH1.2.5/190]

EDWARD, ROBERT, a shoemaker, with his wife Elizabeth Gordon, in Parish of Bellie, 1710. [NAS.CH1.2.29.3/211]

ELLIOT, JOHN, a periwig-maker, a 'papist' in College Kirk parish, Edinburgh, 1704. [NAS.CH1.2.5.2/149]

ELMSLY, GEORGE, groom at Gordon Castle, Morayshire, 1705. [NAS.CH1.2.5/187]

ELMSLY, ISOBEL, wife of Thomas Michy in Alnach, in Glenmuick,Tullich or Glengarden, Aberdeenshire,1718. [NAS.CH1.2.47.271]

EMAN, THOMAS, tenant or cottar in Cargan, Traquair, Dumfries-shire, 1703. [NAS.CH1.2.5.1]

EVANS, Mrs, servant to the Earl of Nithsdale, in Terregles, Dumfries-shire, 1703. [NAS.CH1.2.5.1]

FALCONER, ARCHIBALD, born 1674, from Edinburgh, a student at the Scots College at Douai, 1688. [RSC.I.60]

FALCONER, COSMO, at Ratisbon Seminary in 1719. [SIG#294]

FALCONER, COSMO, born 1723, at the Ratisbon Seminary in 1735. [RSC.I.251]

FALCONER, JOSEPH, from Edinburgh, at the Ratisbon Monastery from 1682, then at Wurzburg from 1695, died in 1732. [SIG#293][SF#272]

FANNING, GEORGE, a Dominican priest in the Hebrides, died at Arisaig in 1678. [IR.XXIV.82]

FARMER, ..., cook to the Marquess of Huntly, parish of Bellie, 1710. [NAS.CH1.2.29.3]

FARQUHAR, AGNES, daughter of John Farquhar, a merchant burgess of Aberdeen, and his deceased wife Catherine Blackhall, in the parish of St Nicolas, Aberdeen, was baptised by Father Robert Francis on 29 September 1696. [SNQ.VIII.181]

FARQUHAR, JOHN, a merchant in Aberdeen, 1704/1705. [NAS.CH1.2.5.2/155]

FARQUHARSON, ALEXANDER, in Strathaven, Banffshire, 1708. [NAS.CH1.2.30/1/28]

FARQUHARSON, ANDREW, born 1740, son of John Farquharson of Alerg and Anna Farquharson, a student at Douai, 1756. [RSC.I.90]

FARQUHARSON, CHARLES, born 1713, son of Lewis Farquharson of Achindryne, studied at Madrid and Douai from 1729, formerly a Jesuit, returned to Scotland in 1745, a Jacobite prisoner in Tilbury, London, 1747, priest in Glenlivet and Braemar, died at Arderg on 30 November 1799. [IR.XVIII.152][Braemar MI][RSC.I.200]

FARQUHARSON, CHARLES, born July 1743, son of John Farquharson of Alerg and Anna Farquharson, a student at Douai, 1756. [RSC.I.90]

FARQUHARSON, CHRISTINE, spouse to Duncan McLauchlane, in Inverchalet, Strathaven, Banffshire, 1708. [NAS.CH1.2.30/1/28]

FARQUHARSON, ELIZABETH, wife of Alexander Michy, in Tullich, Glengarden, Aberdeenshire, 1718. [NAS.CH1.2.47.271]

FARQUHARSON, GEORGE, the elder, of Wester Camdel, and his wife Mary McKenzie, Strathaven, Banffshire, 1708. [NAS.CH1.2.30/1/28]

FARQUHARSON, GREGORY, 4th son of Charles Bui Farquharson, educated at the Scots College in Paris in 1707, died 1746. [SCP#214]

FARQUHARSON, ISABEL, wife to George Bracky NP and Clerk to the Regality of Arbroath, Angus, 1704. [NAS.CH1.2.5.3.186]

FARQUHARSON, ISOBEL, a servant in Balluath, Glenmuick, Aberdeenshire, 1718. [NAS.CH1.2.47.271]

FARQUHARSON, JAMES, in Easter Cambdel, Strathaven, Banffshire, 1708. [NAS.CH1.2.30/1/28]

FARQUHARSON, JAMES, born 23 December 1745, son of Donald Farquharson of Auchreachan and Mary Burnet, a student at Douai, 1768. [RSC.I.91]

FARQUHARSON, JAMES, born 15 March 1746, son of John Farquharson of Alerg and Anna Farquharson, a student at Douai, 1756. [RSC.I.90]

FARQUHARSON, JANET, in Rienamart, widow of Alexander McGregor in Dellovorar, 1767. [NAS.GD248.66.2]

FARQUHARSON, JOHN, of Wester Cambdel, and his wife Helen Ferguson, Strathaven, Banffshire, 1708. [NAS.CH1.2.30/1/28]

FARQUHARSON, JOHN, his wife Janet, and a son and daughter, in Baladan, Glengarden, Aberdeenshire, 1718. [NAS.CH1.2.47.271]

FARQUHARSON, JOHN, born 19 April 1699, son of Lewis Farquharson of Auchindryne, to Douai in 1714, a Jesuit in Tournai in 1718, returned to Scotland in 1729, a missionary in Strathglass, a prisoner in Tilbury, London, 1747, died at Balmoral on 22 August 1782. [IR.XVII.49; XVIII.152; XXIV.95][Braemar MI]

FARQUHARSON, JOHN, born 1728, at Ratisbon Seminary in 1739. [SIG#294][RSC.I.252]

FARQUHARSON, JOHN, Principal of the Scots College at Douai, 1785-1793. [IR.LVIII.223][NLS.Adv.Ms29.3.16/44]

FARQUHARSON, MARGARET, spouse to Duncan Grant in Inver, Strathaven, Banffshire, 1708. [NAS.CH1.2.30/1/28]

FARQUHARSON, ROBERT, the younger of Achriahan, and his wife Margaret Stuart, Strathaven, Banffshire, 1708. [NAS.CH1.2.30/1/28]

FARQUHARSON, ROBERT, second son of Donald Farquharson of Allanaquoich, Aberdeenshire, husband of Mary Gordon, a Jacobite captured at Preston, transported from Liverpool aboard the <u>Anne</u> bound for Virginia on 31 July 1716, returned to Scotland. [JAB.I.73][CTB.XXXI.209][SPAWI.1716.310]

FARQUHARSON, ROBERT, born 28 November 1741, son of Donald Farquharson of Auchreachan and Mary Burnet, a student at Douai, 1755. [RSC.I.90]

FARQUHARSON, WILLIAM, and his wife Christine Farquharson, in Strathaven, Banffshire, 1708. [NAS.CH1.2.30/1/28]

FARQUHARSON, ..., a schoolmaster in Glenlivet, Banffshire, 1720. [NLS.ms68.fo.31-32]

FENDRIGHT, Lady, in College Kirk parish, Edinburgh, 1703.

FERGUSON, ELSPET, in Troquair, Orr, Dumfries-shire, 1705. [NAS.CH1.2.5/156]

FERGUSON, JAMES, in Rigside, Dumfries, 1704. [NAS.CH1.5.2]

FERGUSON, WILLIAM, in Fochabers, 1710. [NAS.CH1.2.29.3/210]

FERRIER, JEAN, daughter of Alexander Ferrier, a skipper in Aberdeen, and Mary More a widow in the parish of St Clement, Fitty, Aberdeen, both Protestants, was baptised by Father Robert Francis on 3 June 1690. [SNQ.VIII.181]

FINDLATOR, MARGARET, servant to the laird of Drum, daughter of the late John Findlator in Burngreen, parish of Methlick, Aberdeenshire, was baptised by Father Robert Francis on 29 March 1698, her godfather was John Francis Stewart the priest's servant. [SNQ.VIII.182]

FINNIE, ALEXANDER, late Curate in Dornoch, an apostate in Ferguson's land at the foot of the Canongait, 'a papist' in Canongait parish, Edinburgh, 1704/1705. [NAS.CH1.2.5.2.149/170]

FINNY, MAC., from Buchan, Aberdeenshire, at the Ratisbon Monastery in 1694. [SIG#293]

FITZGERALD, DAVID, an Irish trader, 'a papist' in Glasgow, 1705. [NAS.CH1.2.5.2.173/2]

FLEMING, CHARLES, born 1675, son of William Fleming, 5th Earl of Wigtown, and Henrietta Seton, educated at the Scots College in Paris from 1687, and at the Scots College at Douai 1689, died in Cumbernauld on 16 May 1747. [NAS.CH1.2.5][SCP#211][RSC.I.60]

FLEMING, DONALD, a servant in Forme(?),in Glenmuick, Tullich, and Glengarden, Aberdeenshire, 1718. [NAS.CH1.2.47/284]

FLEMING, ISOBEL, a widow in Glengarden, Aberdeenshire, with 2 sons 1 daughter, 1718. [NAS.CH1.2.47.271]

FLEMING, JAMES, aged 12, servant to the laird of Kirkconnel, New Abbey, Dumfries-shire, 1703. [NAS.CH1.2.5.1]

FLEMING, Lord JOHN, 6th Earl of Wigtown, born 1673, son of William Fleming, 5th Earl of Wigtown, and his wife Henrietta Seton, educated at the Scots

College in Paris, married (1) Margaret Lindsay, 1698, (2) Mary Keith, 1711, (3) Euphame Lockhart, died in Edinburgh on 10 February 1744. [SCP#211]

FLEMING, JAMES, in Strathaven, Banffshire, 1708. [NAS.CH1.2.30/1/28]

FLEMING, JOHN, and his wife Janet NcWillie, in Strathaven, Banffshire, 1708. [NAS.CH1.2.30/1/28]

FLEMING, P., from Kirkoswald, Ayrshire, at the Ratisbon Monastery from 1669, died 1720. [SIG#293]

FLEMING, WILLIAM, tenant in Buss of Kirkconnel, with his daughter Elizabeth aged 18, son William aged 14, New Abbey, Dumfries-shire, 1703. [NAS.CH1.2.5.1]

FLEMING, WILLIAM, and his wife Janet McCuck, in Criusley, Strathaven, Banffshire, 1708. [NAS.CH1.2.30/1/28]

FORBES, ALEXANDER, a barber in Aberdeen, 1704/1705. [NAS.CH1.2.5.2/155]

FORBES, ALEXANDER, in Comry, in Ruthven, Strathbogie,1710. [NAS.CH1.2.29.3/209]

FORBES, CHARLES, born 1742, a student at Douai, 1752. [RSC.I.89]

FORBES, ELSPET, a servant in the parish of Bellie, 1710. [NAS.CH1.2.29.3]

FORBES, GEORGE, son of George Forbes and Elizabeth Leslie, a student at Douai, 1742. [RSC.I.85]

FORBES, GEORGE, son of George Forbes of Skellatur and Christine Gordon, a student at Douai, 1750. [RSC.I.88]

FORBES, ISOBEL, servant in Fochabers, Morayshire, 1705. [NAS.CH1.2.5/2, 187]

FORBES, JAMES, servant in Landends, Parish of Bellie, 1710. [NAS.CH1.2.29.3/211]

FORBES, JANET, in Fochabers, Morayshire, 1705. [NAS.CH1.2.5/2]

FORBES, JEAN, daughter of Thomas Forbes of Robslaw and his wife Jean Jamieson in St Nicolas parish, Aberdeen, was baptised on 20 November 1687 by Father Robert Francis in Aberdeen, godfather Alexander Irvine of Lairny and godmother Mrs Jean Irvine daughter to the late laird of Drum, both in St Nicolas. [NNQ.VIII.180]

FORBES, JEAN, servant in Fetteresso, Kincardineshire, 1704. [NAS.CH1.2.5.3/201]

FORBES, JEAN, wife to Walter Angus, Parish of Bellie, 1710. [NAS.CH1.2.29.3/211]

FORBES, JOHN, born 1737, son of George Forbes of Skellatur and Christine Gordon, a student at Douai, 1749. [RSC.I.86]

FORBES, KATRINE, in Ardach, in Glenmuick, Tullich, and Glengarden, Aberdeenshire, 1718. [NAS.CH1.2.47/284]

FORBES, MARGARET, in Fochabers, Morayshire, 1705. [NAS.CH1.2.5/2]

FORBES, NATHANIEL, born 1739, son of George Forbes of Skellatur and Christine Gordon, a student at Douai, 1750. [RSC.I.88]

FORBES, ROBERT, a servant in Fochabers, Morayshire, 1705. [NAS.CH1.2.5/2]

FORBES, ROBERT, and his sister Janet Forbes wife of Walter Angus a wright in Fochabers, Morayshire, 1705. [NAS.CH1.2.5/187]

FORBES, ROBERT, with his wife Janet Sinclair, and son John, in Wallheads, parish of Bellie, 1710. [NAS.CH1.2.29.3]

FORBES, ROBERT, servant to the Marquess of Huntly, parish of Bellie, 1710. [NAS.CH1.2.29.3]

FORBES, ROBERT, born 1739, a student at Douai, 1753. [RSC.I.89]

FORBES, THOMAS, of Robslaw, Aberdeen, 1704/1705. [NAS.CH1.2.5.2/155]

FORBES, WALTER, in Ruthven, Strathbogie,1710. [NAS.CH1.2.29.3/209]

FORBES, WILLIAM, son of George Forbes of Skellatur and Christine Gordon, a student at Douai, 1749. [RSC.I.87]

FORDYCE, FRANCIS, born 1682, son of John Fordyce, a student at the Scots College at Douai, 1695, died in Spain. [RSC.I.64]

FORDYCE, ISABEL, servant to the laird of Kirkconnel, New Abbey, Dumfries-shire, 1703. [NAS.CH1.2.5.1]

FORDYCE, ..., a priest in Aberdeen, 1714. [NLS.ms976.143]

FORRESTER, ALEXANDER, born in Cromarty in 1701, ordained in Rome in 1732, a priest in Uist, died there in December 1780. [IR.XVIII.135]

FORRETT, ANNE, with her son William, Parish of Bellie, 1710. [NAS.CH1.2.29.3/211]

FORSYTH, ALEXANDER, at the Ratisbon Seminary in 1748. [SIG#295][RSC.I.252]

FORSYTH, HENRY, born 1702, a former Jesuit, died in Braemar, Aberdeenshire, on 19 November 1780. [IR.XVIII.155][Braemar MI]

FORSYTH, MARGARET, in Richorne, Orr, Dumfries-shire, 1705. [NAS.CH1.2.5/156]

FRASER, ALEXANDER, of Kinnaries, Strathglass, Inverness-shire, educated at Douai from 1663, an apostate in Kiltarlity, 1679; liberated in Inverness 1690. [IR.XXIV.78/82]; 1685, 1703. [NAS.GD23.10.226][RPCS.XV.178]

FRASER, ALEXANDER, at the Ratisbon Seminary in 1800. [SIG#295][RSC.I.254]

FRASER, CHARLES, at the Ratisbon Seminary in 1756. [SIG#295][RSC.I.252]

FRASER, CHARLES, at the Ratisbon Seminary in 1800, a missionary in Aberdeen 1830. [SIG#295][RSC.I.254]

FRASER, HUGH, of Kinneras, Kiltarlity, Inverness-shire, 1710. [NAS.CH1.2.29.3]

FRASER, HUGH, a former Captain of the 78th [Fraser's Highlanders] Regiment, a land grant in New York in 1773. [PCCol#5/597]

FRASER, JOHN, of Gardinmore, Inverness-shire, 1703.

FRASER, JOHN, son of William Fraser and Margaret McDonald, a student at Douai, 1742. [RSC.I.85]

FRASER, JOHN, son of John Fraser of Glenvackie, Strathglass, and Margaret Chisholm, from Strathglass to Madrid, from there to Douai in 1734, a Jesuit in Bordeaux 1738, died as a missionary in Parton, Galloway, 1797. [IR.XXIV.94][RSC.I.200]

FRASER, JOHN, a former Captain of the 78th [Fraser's Highlanders] Regiment, a land grant in New York in 1773. [PCCol#5/597]

FRASER, PETER, educated at the Scots College in Paris from 1696 to 1702, ordained at Scothouse on 11 March 1704, a priest in Strathaven, Banffshire, 1710, died at Morar on 9 March 1731. [NAS.CH1.2.30/1/5][SCP#212][IR.LV.206]

FRASER, SIMON, in Kulmaskiak, an apostate in Kiltarlity, 1679. [IR.XXIV.82]

FRASER, SIMON, son of William Fraser of Guisachan, Strathglass, and Margaret McDonnell, educated at Douai 1743, a Captain of the 78th [Fraser's Highlanders] Regiment, settled in Bennington, New York, by 1773, husband of Isabella Grant, parents of William, Angus, and Simon, died in Albany, New York, 1770s. [PCCol.5/597][RSC.I.85]

FULLERTON, THOMAS, a weaver in Glen Ogilvie, Angus, 1704. [NAS.CH1.2.5/204]

FYFE, THOMAS, born 17 March 1674, son of William Fyfe and Helen Gordon in Aberdeen, a student at the Scots College at Douai, 1681; rector of the Scots College in Madrid, 1715-1725. [RSC.I.61/203]

FYFFE, Mrs, in Cross Close, Old Kirk parish, Edinburgh, 1703. [NAS.CH1.2.5.2/151]

GAIRDEN, ALEXANDER, born 1742, son of John Gairden of Bellamore and Isabella Smith, a student at Douai 1753. [RSC.I.89]

GAIRDEN, CHARLES, son of John Gairden of Bellamore and Isabella Smith, a student at Douai 1753. [RSC.I.89]

GAIRDN, JAMES, and his wife Giles Morison, at the Raws of Huntly, Dunbennan parish, 1710. [NAS.CH1.2.29.3/210]

GAIRN, HELEN, tenant, Parish of Bellie, 1710. [NAS.CH1.2.29.3/211]

GAIRN, MARY, a servant in Nether Achinroth, in the parish of Bellie, 1710. [NAS.CH1.2.29.3/211]

GALL, LILIAS, at the Raws of Huntly, Dunbennan parish, 1710. [NAS.CH1.2.29.3/210]

GALLAN, JAMES, tenant in Wallheads, with sons George and John, parish of Bellie, 1710. [NAS.CH1.2.29.3]

GALLON, JOHN, a laborer in Fochabers, Morayshire, and his wife Jean Livingstone, Morayshire, 1705; a tenant in Fochabers, 1710. [NAS.CH1.2.5/2; 2.29.3/210]

GALLOWAY, MAGNUS, in Bowhouse, Terregles, Dumfries-shire, 1703. [NAS.CH1.2.5.1]

GALLOWAY, MAGNUS, and Mary Irving in Kirklands, Terregles and Kirkgunzeon, Dumfries-shire, 1705. [NAS.CH1.2.5.2]

GARDEN, JOHN, a shoemaker in Banff, Banffshire, 1794. [NAS.SC2.72.4]

GARDYNE, BETHIA, spouse to Charles Gardyne of Ballashein, Aboyne or Glentanar, Aberdeenshire, 1704, 1710. [NAS.CH1.2.5/190; CH1.2.29.3]

GARDYNE, ELIZABETH, in Aboyne or Glentanar, 1710. [NAS.CH1.2.29.3]

GARDYNE, JOHN, in Inverhalt, Aboyne or Glentanar, Aberdeenshire, 1704. [NAS.CH1.2.5/190]

GARDYNE, JOHN, of Ballamore, living in Braeline, Glentanar, Aberdeenshire, and his sister Elisabeth Gardyne, 1704; with his wife Katherine Elphinstone and son John, 1710. [NAS.CH1.2.5/190; CH1.2.29.3]

GARMONACH, MARJORY, a servant in Strathaven, Banffshire, 1708, [NAS.CH1.2.30/1/28]

GARTLAY, THOMAS, son of Alexander Gartlay, a pilot, and his wife Marjorie Gayen, both Protestants, was baptised in Aberdeen by Father Robert Francis on 27 November 1687, godfather was Thomas Forbes of Robslaw, and godmother was Sara Blackburn wife of Alexander Ross a painter, both Catholics in St Nicolas, Aberdeen. [SNQ.VIII.180]

GEDDES, ALEXANDER, born 1737 at Pathhead near Preshome, son of Alexander Geddes and Janet Mitchell, educated at the Scots College in Paris 1758, ordained in Paris 1764, died in London 20 February 1802. [SCP#218]

GEDDES, ANDREW, a tenant in Tynett, with his wife Isobel Geddes, in the parish of Bellie, 1710. [NAS.CH1.2.29.3/211]

GEDDES, ANNE, in Tullo, Parish of Bellie, 1710. [NAS.CH1.2.29.3/211]

GEDDES, GEORGE, a tenant, with daughter Isobel, parish of Bellie, 1710. [NAS.CH1.2.29.3]

GEDDES, JEAN, in Ryfinn, parish of Bellie, 1710. [NAS.CH1.2.29.3]

GEDDES, JOHN, a student at the Scots College in Valladolid, 1769. [SC.I.204]

GEDDES, JOHN, born 29 August 1735 at the Mains of Corridoun, Enzie, Banffshire, ordained in Rome 1759, in Dickson's Close, Edinburgh, 1785, and in Black Friars Wynd, Edinburgh, 1790/1791. [SCA.BL.3.451.10; BL.4.32.10/11]; Bishop John Geddes, died 11 February 1799. [Snow Kirkyard, Aberdeen, MI] [CDS]

GEDDES, LILLIAS, Parish of Bellie, 1710. [NAS.CH1.2.29.3/211]

GEDDES, MARGARET, in Ruthven, Strathbogie,1710. [NAS.CH1.2.29.3/209]

GEDDES, MARGARET, Parish of Bellie, 1710. [NAS.CH1.2.29.3/211]

GEDDES, WILLIAM, servant to George Anderson in Nether Dallachie, in the parish of Bellie, 1710. [NAS.CH1.2.29.3/211]

GEDDES, WILLIAM, tenant in Boghead, and wife Elspet Robertson, parish of Bellie, 1710. [NAS.CH1.2.29.3]

GEORGE, BEATRIX, spouse to Patrick Siboall (?) a skinner in Dalkeith, 'a papist' in the Regality of Dalkeith, Midlothian, 1705. [NAS.CH1.2.5.2.169]

GEORGE, CHARLES, a manufacturer in Keith, Banffshire, 1794. [NAS.SC2.72.4]

GEORGE, ELIZABETH, spouse to Patrick Steel in Dalkeith, Midlothian, 1705. [NAS.CH1.2.5/182]

GEORGE, FRANCIS, his wife, and two children, 'papists' in Canongait parish, Edinburgh, 1705. [NAS.CH1.2.5.2.170]

GEORGE, JAMES, a manufacturer in Keith, Banffshire, 1794. [NAS.SC2.72.4]

GEORGE, JOHN, a tailor in Aberdeen, 1704/1705. [NAS.CH1.2.5.2/155]

GEORGE, JOHN, in Tillilermond, in Ruthven, Strathbogie,1710. [NAS.CH1.2.29.3/209]

GEORGE, MARGARET, in Echt, Aberdeenshire, 1704, 1710. [NAS.CH1.2.5.3.194; CH1.2.29.3]

GEORGE, MARION, in Echt, Aberdeenshire, 1704. [NAS.CH1.2.5.3.194]

GIBB, ALEXANDER, born 1671, from Aberdeen, a student at the Scots College at Douai, 1685. [RSC.I.58]

GIBB, ALEXANDER, born around 1611, a merchant in Aberdeen, transported to Edinburgh Tolbooth, 1681. [RPCS.VII.739]

GIBB, ALEXANDER, a merchant in Aberdeen, 1704/1705. [NAS.CH1.2.5.2/155]

GIBB, ANDREW, a weaver in Fochabers, 1710. [NAS.CH1.2.29.3/210]

GIBB, ISOBEL, in Ruthven, Strathbogie,1710. [NAS.CH1.2.29.3/209]

GIBB, JAMES, tenant in Wallheads, parish of Bellie, 1710. [NAS.CH1.2.29.3]

GIBB, JAMES, a servant, in Fochabers, 1710. [NAS.CH1.2.29.3/210]

GIBBONACH, ELSPET, a widow in Strathaven, Banffshire, 1708. [NAS.CH1.2.30/1/28]

GIBSON, MARGARET, in Balloch, Auchterarder, Perthshire,1703. [NAS.CH1.2.5.2]

GLADSTANES, WILLIAM, in Carruchen, Troquair, Orr, Dumfries-shire, 1705. [NAS.CH1.2.5/156]

GLASS, WILLIAM, in Inverchabel, Strathaven, Banffshire, 1708. [NAS.CH1.2.30/1/28]

GLASSELL, JANET, a widow in Cargan, and her children Janet Edgar, John Edgar, and Robert Edgar, in Troquair, Orr, Dumfries-shire, 1705. [NAS.CH1.2.5/156]

GLENDINNING, AGNES, relict of the late Homer Maxwell of Milnhead Kirkmahoe, Dumfries-shire, 1705. [NAS.CH1.2.5.1]

GLENDINNING, ALEXANDER, at the Mill of Maryculter, Kincardineshire, 1705. [NAS.CH1.2.5.2]

GLENDENNING, CHARLES, born 1746, a stuent at Douai, 1759. [RSC.I.91]

GLENDINNING, ELIZABETH, relict of Thomas Maxwell of Gelston, in Buittle, Kirkcudbrightshire, 1705. [NAS.CH1.2.5.2]

GLENDENNING, JAMES, born 7 September 1744, a student at Douai 1757. [RSC.I.90]

GLENDINNING, ROBERT, of Parton, with his wife Agnes Herries, and son George, in Parton, Kirkcudbrightshire, 1705. [NAS.CH1.2.5.2]

GLENDINNING, ROBERT, son of Robert Glendinning and Mary Neilson, a student at Douai, 1750. [RSC.I.87]

GLENDINNING, WILLIAM, son of Robert Glendinning and Mary Neilson, a student at Douai, 1750. [RSC.I.87]

GODSMAN, JAMES, a heritor of Parish of Bellie, with his wife Hendrietta Dunbar,and their daughters Isobel and Marjory, 1710. [NAS.CH1.2.29.3/211]

GODSMAN, JOHN, was sent abroad for education in 1719. [NLS.ms68.31-32]

GOLD, GEORGE, and his wife Beatrix Doig, in Ruthven, Strathaven, Banffshire, 1708. [NAS.CH1.2.30/1/28]

GOLD, JAMES, and his wife Janet Stuart, in Strathaven, Banffshire, 1708. [NAS.CH1.2.30/1/28]

GOODWINN, Mrs, a schoolmistress in Edinburgh, 1703. [NAS.CH1.2.5.2/153]

GOODWYND, JOHN, servant to the Marquess of Huntly, parish of Bellie, 1710. [NAS.CH1.2.29.3]

GORDON, the DUCHESS of, and her daughter Lady Jean Gordon, 'papists' in the Canongait, Edinburgh, 1703/1704. [NAS.CH1.2.5.2/149/151]

GORDON, the DUKE of, lodging in the Citadel, North Leith, Edinburgh, a 'papist', 1704; at Gordon Castle, Morayshire, 1705. [NAS.CH1.2.5.2.149; CH1.2.5.187]

GORDON, ADAM, in the Mylne of Smythston, Rhynie, with his wife Jean Gordon and their young children, 1710. [NAS.CH1.2.29.3/209]

GORDON, AGNES, Lady Wauchop, in Crossmichael, Kirkcudbrightshire, 1705. [NAS.CH1.2.5.2]

GORDON, AGNES, in the parish of Bellie, 1710. [NAS.CH1.2.29.3/211]

GORDON, ALEXANDER, son of John Gordon of Seaton, a Protestant in Old Aberdeen, and his wife Bettie Irvine, a Catholic, was baptised a Protestant by John Reith minister of Old Aberdeen, on 15 June 1688, 'the same day at the desire of the said Bettie and her Catholic relations' the child was baptised as a Catholic, the godfather was Alexander Irvine of Lairny, and the godmother was Margaret Aedie wife of Richard Irvine of Carnfield, both in the parish of St Nicolas. [SNQ.VII.180]

GORDON, ALEXANDER, of Easter Cambdel, his wife Giles McDonald, and their daughter Katharine Gordon, in Strathaven, Banffshire, 1708. [NAS.CH1.2.30/1/28]

GORDON, ALEXANDER, of Balnacraig, with his wife Catherine Dixon, in Aboyne or Glentanar, 1710. [NAS.CH1.2.29.3]

GORDON, ALEXANDER, grieve to Huntly, and his wife Anne Lumsdale, in Fochabers, 1710. [NAS.CH1.2.29.3/210]

GORDON, ALEXANDER, and his wife Isobel Gordon, at the Raws of Huntly, Dunbennan parish, 1710. [NAS.CH1.2.29.3/210]

GORDON, ALEXANDER, of Achintowell, an apostate in Aberchirder, and his daughter Mary, 1710. [NAS.CH1.2.29.3]

GORDON, Major ALEXANDER, in Glenmuick, Aberdeenshire,1718. [NAS.CH1.2.47.271]

GORDON, ALEXANDER, at the Ratisbon Seminary in 1718. [SIG#294][RSC.I.250]

GORDON, ALEXANDER, from Dorleathers, at the Ratisbon Seminary in 1719. [SIG#294][RSC.I.251]

GORDON, ALEXANDER, of Cuffurich, born 3 November 1710, educated at the Scots College in Paris 1724, deacon at Scalan 1734, ordained 1734, died in Edinburgh on 9 November 1793. [SCP#215]

GORDON, ALEXANDER, of Licheston, at the Ratisbon Seminary in 1739. [SIG#294][RSC.I.252]

GORDON, ALEXANDER, from Newmills, Keith, educated at the Scots College in Paris around 1749, ordained 1764, died at Traquair on 1 October 1818. [SCP#217]

GORDON, ANDREW, at the Ratisbon Monastery in 1732. [SIG#294]

GORDON, ANNA, servant or gentlewoman to Lady Jean Semple, in Edinburgh, 'a papist' living in Main's land immediately below the Half-Moon, College Kirk parish, Edinburgh, 1704/1705. [NAS.CH1.2.5.2.149/171]

GORDON, ANNA, servant to the Countess of Marischal, in Fetteresso, Kincardineshire, 1704. [NAS.CH1.2.5.3/201]

GORDON, ANNA, in Fochabers, Morayshire, 1705. [NAS.CH1.2.5/2]

GORDON, ANNA, wife of George Gibb in Lomond, Kinnoir parish, 1710. [NAS.CH1.2.29.3/210]

GORDON, ANNE, with her sons Charles Leslie, aged four, and Robert Leslie, aged two, in Echt, Aberdeenshire, 1704, 1710. [NAS.CH1.2.5.3.194; CH1.2.29.3]

GORDON, ANS., son of Alexander Gordon in Kinquidy, Diocese of Aberdeen, at the Ratisbon Monastery in 1682, died 1702. [SIG#293]

GORDON, ANSELM, born 1672, at Wurzburg Monastery in 1689, died 1730. [SF#281]

GORDON, ARTHUR, born 1731, son of Lord Baldony, at the Ratisbon Seminary, 1739. [SIG#294][RSC.I.252]

GORDON, AUGUSTINE, at Wurzburg in 1686. [SF#272]

GORDON, CHARLES, born 1670, son of Charles Gordon, Earl of Aboyne, and Elizabeth Lyon, daughter of the Earl of Kinghorn and Strathmore, a student at the Scots College at Douai, 1681. [RSC.I.55]

GORDON, CHARLES, of Tilliquhodie, now in Lonbride, Morayshire, 1705. [NAS.CH1.2.5/2]

GORDON, CHARLES, of Achanachy, Ruthven, Strathbogie, 1710. [NAS.CH1.2.29.3/209]

GORDON, CHARLES, of Baldorny, born 1737, at the Ratisbon Seminary in 1748. [SIG#295][RSC.I.252]

GORDON, ELIZABETH, in Robestoun, Kinnoir parish, 1710. [NAS.CH1.2.29.3/210]

GORDON, FRANCIS, born 3 April 1693, son of John Gordon of Dunmeath, a Protestant, and Anna Gordon, a Catholic, was baptised on 8 April 1693 by Father Robert Francis. [SNQ.VIII.181]

GORDON, FRANCIS, and his wife residing in the Duke of Gordon's lodging in the Citadel of Leith, Edinburgh, 1704. [NAS.CH1.2.5.2.149]

GORDON, FRANCIS, born 1742, son of ....Gordon of Kenmore, a student at Douai, 1751. [RSC.I.88]

GORDON, GEORGE, a merchant in Aberdeen, 1704.[NAS.CH1.2.5/155]

GORDON, GEORGE, son of Lord Alexander of Auchintoul and Isabel Gray in the dioceses of Aberdeen, educated at the Scots College in Paris in 1684, married Barbara Mackenzie, died at sea 1746. [SCP#211]

GORDON, GEORGE, born 1675, a student at the Scots College at Douai, 1685. [RSC.I.58]

GORDON, GEORGE, a gentleman at Gordon Castle, Morayshire, 1705. [NAS.CH1.2.5/187]

GORDON, GEORGE, in Monidie, son of Alexander Gordon of Achintowell, and his wife Barbara McKenzie, in Aberchirder, 1710. [NAS.CH1.2.29.3]

GORDON, GEORGE, of Sueltoun, chamberlain to the Marquess of Huntly, and his wife Jean Lesly, parish of Bellie, 1710. [NAS.CH1.2.29.3]

GORDON, GEORGE, son of J. Gordon of Beldormie and Mary Gordon, educated at the Scots College in Paris, 1735-1742, later an apprentice ship-carpenter in Leith. [SCP#216]

GORDON, GEORGE, born 1740, died 10 May 1805. [Bellie Tynet gravestone]

GORDON, GEORGE, born 1776, a student at the Scots College at Valladolid, 1788, a missionary in Auchendown, died in Dufftown on 10 May 1856. [SC.I.210]

GORDON, HELEN, in Ruthven, Strathbogie,1710. [NAS.CH1.2.29.3/209]

GORDON, HELEN, Parish of Bellie, 1710. [NAS.CH1.2.29.3/211]

GORDON, ISOBEL, a 'papist' in Liberton, Edinburgh, 1704. [NAS.CH1.2.5.2.149]

GORDON, ISABELL, servant to the Duchess of Gordon, 'a papist' in Canongait, Edinburgh, 1705. [NAS.CH1.2.5.2.170]

GORDON, ISABEL, in Ruthven, Strathbogie,1710. [NAS.CH1.2.29.3/209]

GORDON, JAMES, tenant and wadsetter of Kirkbride, and his children Janes aged 22, James aged 20, Elizabeth aged 18, and a daughter aged 13, in Kirkpatrick-Durham, Dumfries-shire, 1703. [NAS.CH1.2.5.1]

GORDON, JAMES, in Fochabers, Morayshire, 1705; a quarrier in Fochabers, and his wife Isobel Cuie, 1710. [NAS.CH1.2.5/2; 2.29.3/210]

GORDON, JAMES, servant to the Earl of Nithsdale, in Terregles, Dumfries-shire, 1703. [NAS.CH1.2.5.1]

GORDON, JAMES, servant to the Earl of Nithsdale, and his wife Isabel Hepburn, and daughter Anna Gordon, living at Bull's Close, 'papists' in New Kirk parish, Edinburgh, 1704/1705. [NAS.CH1.2.5.2.149; 175/1]

GORDON, JAMES, a grieve in Terregles, Dumfries-shire, 1705. [NAS.CH1.2.5.2]

GORDON, JAMES, in Easter Cambdel, Strathaven, Banffshire, 1708. [NAS.CH1.2.30/1/28]

GORDON, JAMES, son of Lord Achintoull, in Aberchirder, 1710. [NAS.CH1.2.29.3]

GORDON, JAMES, son of Alexander Gordon of Dorlaithers and Helen Irvine, a student at Douai, 1751. [RSC.I.88]

GORDON, JAMES, of Auchleuchries, died in the Scots College in Paris on 3 September 1762. [SCP#218]

GORDON, JANET, a servant in Dryburn, parish of Bellie, 1710. [NAS.CH1.2.29.3]

GORDON, Mrs JEAN, servant to the laird of Drum, Aberdeenshire, daughter of John Gordon of Culter, was baptised by Father Robert Francis in the parish of Dalmaik on 29 March 1698. [SNQ.VIII.182]

GORDON, JEAN, a gentlewoman, in Canongait, 1703. [NAS.CH1.2.5.2/151]

GORDON, JEAN, servant to James Brown a surgeon, 'a papist' in Greyfriars Kirk parish, Edinburgh, 1704/1705. [NAS.CH1.2.5.2.149;175/1]

GORDON, JEAN, relict of Glencat, with two children, Aboyne or Glentanar, 1710. [NAS.CH1.2.29.3]

GORDON, JEAN, teacher at a girls' school, in Fochabers, 1710. [NAS.CH1.2.29.3/210]

GORDON, JOHN, a student at the Scots College at Douai, 1685. [RSC.I.58]

GORDON, JOHN, a widower in Coulter, parish of Peterculter, was rebaptised by Father Robert Francis on 20 January 1698. [SNQ.VIII.182]

GORDON, JOHN, servant to the Duchess of Gordon, 'a papist' in Canongait, Edinburgh, 1703/1704/ 1705. [NAS.CH1.2.5.2.149/151/170]

GORDON, JOHN, born in 1704 at Glencat, Birse, Aberdeenshire, son of John Gordon of Glencat and Jean Gordon of Barrack. [IR.LV.206]

GORDON, JOHN, son of Patrick Gordon of Harlaw, Aberdeen, 1704. [NAS.CH1.2.5/155]

GORDON, JOHN, and his wife Janet Gordon, in Strathaven, Banffshire, 1708. [NAS.CH1.2.30/1/28]

GORDON, JOHN, priest in the parish of Bellie, Banffshire, 1710. [NAS.CH1.2.30/1/5][NLS.ms68.31-32]

GORDON, JOHN, servant to the Marquess of Huntly, parish of Bellie, 1710. [NAS.CH1.2.29.3]

GORDON, JOHN, in Ruthven, Strathbogie,1710. [NAS.CH1.2.29.3/209]

GORDON, JOHN, and his wife Jean Gordon, in Cormollet, Ruthven, Strathbogie,1710. [NAS.CH1.2.29.3/209]

GORDON, JOHN, son of Alexander Gordon of Dorlaithers and Helen Irvine, a student at Douai, 1748. [RSC.I.86]

GORDON, JOHN BAPTIST, born 1749 at Newmill, Keith, educated at the Scots College in Paris and at Valladolid 1770, ordained there in 1771, died in a mental hospital. [SCP#218][RSC.I.204]

GORDON, JOHN, a student at the Scots College at Valladolid, 1774, died 1823. [RSC.I.206]

GORDON, KATHERINE, wife to John Taylor, and their daughter Isobel, in Landends, Parish of Bellie, 1710. [NAS.CH1.2.29.3/211]

GORDON, MARGARET, (1), was born on 7 July 1691, daughter of John Gordon of Seaton, a Protestant, and his wife Bettie Irvine, a Catholic, was baptised a Protestant on 9 July 1691, and as a Catholic on 5 August 1691 by Father Robert Francis. [SNQ.VIII.181]

GORDON, MARGARET, (2), was born on 7 July 1691, daughter of John Gordon of Seaton, a Protestant, and his wife Bettie Irvine, a Catholic, was baptised a

Protestant in 1696, and as a Catholic on 1 October 1696 by Father Robert Francis. [SNQ.VIII.182]

GORDON, MARGARET, sister to the late John Gordon of Rothiemay, Rothiemay, Strathbogie, 1710. [NAS.CH1.2.29.3]

GORDON, MARJORY, a servant to the Duchess of Gordon, a 'papist' in the Canongait, 1703/1704. [NAS.CH1.2.5.2/149/151]

GORDON, MARY, sister to James Gordon of Letterfourie, and wife to John Duff, died at Foggyloan near Auchentoul in April 1782. [IR.XVII.46]

GORDON, MAY, sister to the late John Gordon of Rothiemay, and spouse of John Ogilvie of Rotnodie, Rothiemay, Strathbogie, 1710. [NAS.CH1.2.29.3]

GORDON, MUIREAL, Tullich, Aberdeenshire, 1718. [NAS.CH1.2.7.271]

GORDON, PATRICK, born 1672, son of Charles Gordon, Earl of Aboyne, and Elizabeth Lyon, daughter of the Earl of Kinghorn and Strathmore, a student at the Scots College at Douai, 1681. [RSC.I.55]

GORDON, PATRICK, son of William Gordon of Kirkhill, Aberdeen, 1704. [NAS.CH1.2.5/155]

GORDON, PATRICK, of Cults, Aberdeen, 1705. [NAS.CH1.2.5.2/155]

GORDON, PATRICK, of Harlaw, and his sons John and William, Aberdeen, 1705. [NAS.CH1.2.5.2/155]

GORDON, PATRICK, of Letterfury, at the Ratisbon Seminary in 1718. [RSC.I.250]

GORDON, PATRICK, of Aberlour, Banffshire, 1793.[NAS.SC2.72.4]

GORDON, PETER, a hat-maker in Fochabers, 1710. [NAS.CH1.2.29.3/210]

GORDON, PETER, a servant in Fochabers, 1710. [NAS.CH1.2.29.3/210]

GORDON, Father PETER, a priest in London, a Jacobite transported to Holland in 1746. [SHS.II.240]

GORDON, Monsignor ROBERT, born 1668, son of Robert Gordon in Aberdeen, a student at the Scots College at Douai, 1693. [RSC.I.62]

GORDON, ROBERT, a merchant in Fochabers, Morayshire, his wife Isobel Reid, Morayshire, 1705. [NAS.CH1.2.5/2]

GORDON, ROBERT, a Jesuit priest in the Presbytery of Dingwall, son of the late John Gordon sometime incumbent at Killearn, 1707. [NAS.CH1.2/30/1/4][NLS.ms68.31-32]

GORDON, ROBERT, in Cross, Kinnore parish, 1710. [NAS.CH1.2.29.3/210]

GORDON, ROBERT, at the Ratisbon Seminary in 1719. [SIG.294][RSC.I.250]

GORDON, SICILIE, Parish of Bellie, 1710. [NAS.CH1.2.29.3/211]

GORDON, THOMAS, a merchant in Fochabers, Morayshire, with his wife Isobel Reid and son Robert Gordon, 1705, 1710. [NAS.CH1.2.5/2,187; 2.29.3/210]

GORDON, THOMAS, a widower in Cromchlaggin, Strathaven, Banffshire, 1708. [NAS.CH1.2.30/1/28]

GORDON, THOMAS, a stocking weaver in Banff, 1794. [NAS.SC2.72.4]

GORDON, VIOLET, spouse to William McPherson in Strathaven, Banffshire, 1708. [NAS.CH1.2.30/1/28]

GORDON, WILLIAM, son of Patrick Gordon of Harlaw, Aberdeen, 1704. [NAS.CH1.2.5/155]

GORDON, WILLIAM, of Kirkhill, and his son Patrick, Aberdeen, 1704/1705. [NAS.CH1.2.5.2/155]

GORDON, WILLIAM, servant to the Duchess of Gordon, 'a papist' in Canongait, Edinburgh, 1705. [NAS.CH1.2.5.2.170]

GORDON, WILLIAM, groom at Gordon Castle, Morayshire, 1705. [NAS.CH1.2.5/187]

GORDON, WILLIAM, and his wife Jean McDonald, Strathaven, Banffshire, 1708. [NAS.CH1.2.30/1/28]

GORDON, WILLIAM, with his wife Janet Gordon, in Tulloches, in Ruthven, Strathbogie,1710. [NAS.CH1.2.29.3/209]

GORDON, WILLIAM, at the Raws of Huntly, Dunbennan parish, 1710. [NAS.CH1.2.29.3/210]

GORDON, WILLIAM, at the Ratisbon Seminary, 1713. [SIG#294][RSC.I.250]

GORDON, WILLIAM, son of Francis Gordon of Craig, a student at the Scots College in Madrid, 1715. [RSC.I.200]

GORDON, WILLIAM, late in Inlanden of Enzie, died in April 1775, husband of Jean Anderson, died 1759. [Bellie Tynet gravestone]

GORDON, WILLIAM, a farmer in Kempcairn, Banffshire, 1794. [NAS.SC2.72.4]

GORDON, Miss, of Auchentool, 1773. [NAS.GD44.4399.14]

GORDON, Misses, of Beldornie, residing in St Andrews, 1782. [IR.XVII.77]

GRAHAM, CHARLES, at Ratisbon Seminary in 1779. [SIG#295][RSC.I.253]

GRAHAM, MARY, a tenant in Gaidon, in Buittle, Kirkcudbrightshire, 1705. [NAS.CH1.2.5.2]

GRAHAM, PATRICK, son of Colonel Peter Graham, a student at the Scots College at Douai, 1696. [RSC.I.64]

GRAHAM, THOMAS, born 1766, at the Ratisbon Seminary in 1775. [SIG.295][RSC.I.253]

GRANT, ALEXANDER, born 1680, son of William Grant of Crichy, a student at the Scots College at Douai, 1693. [RSC.I.62]

GRANT, ALEXANDER, servant to the Niddrie family, and his spouse Isobel Gordon, 'papists' in Liberton, Edinburgh, 1704. [NAS.CH1.2.5.2.149]

GRANT, ALEXANDER, of Glenconglass, and his wife Margaret Gordon, in Strathaven, Banffshire, 1708. [NAS.CH1.2.30/1/28]

GRANT, ALEXANDER, in Strathaven, Banffshire, 1708. [NAS.CH1.2.30/1/28]

GRANT, ALEXANDER, at the Ratisbon Seminary, 1718. [SIG#294][RSC.I.250]

GRANT, ALEXANDER, at the Ratisbon Seminary, 1739. [SIG#294][RSC.I.252]

GRANT, ALEXANDER, a student at the Scots College at Valladolid, 1771, died in April 1774. [RSC.I.205]

GRANT, ANNA, spouse to John Grant in Acharahan, Strathaven, Banffshire, 1708. [NAS.CH1.2.30/1/28]

GRANT, ANNE, in the parish of Bellie, 1710. [NAS.CH1.2.29.3/211]

GRANT, CALUM, from Strathdon, son of the laird of Ruthven, at the Ratisbon Seminary, 1721. [SIG#294][RSC.I.250]

GRANT, DUNCAN, and his wife Bettie Watson, at the Raws of Huntly, Dunbennan parish, 1710. [NAS.CH1.2.29.3/210]

GRANT, E., from Strathdon, at Ratisbon Monastery, 1720. [SIG#293]

GRANT, HELEN, of Storine, in Glengarden, Aberdeenshire, 1718. [NAS.CH1.2.47.271]

GRANT, JAMES, a tenant in Nether Dallachie, with his wife Marjory Bremner, in the parish of Bellie, 1710. [NAS.CH1.2.29.3/211]

GRANT, JAMES, son of a farmer at Wester Boggs, Enzie, Banffshire, ordained in Rome during 1734, priest in Lochaber, Uist, and Barra, later bishop, died in Aberdeen 3 December 1778. [IR.XVIII.136][Snow Kirkyard, Aberdeen, MI]

GRANT, JOHN, born 15 August 1672, son of Peter Grant of Caron and .... Dunbar, a student at the Scots College at Douai, 1695. [RSC.I.63]

GRANT, JOHN, born 1685, son of John Grant of Ballindaloch, a student at the Scots College at Douai, 1695. [RSC.I.64]

GRANT, JOHN, servant to the late William Thomson, 'a papist' in Canongait, Edinburgh, 1703/1704/1705. [NAS.CH1.2.5.2.149/170]

GRANT, JOHN, the elder, of Achiahan, and his wife Anna McGregor, Strathaven, Banffshire, 1708. [NAS.CH1.2.30/1/28]

GRANT, or MCGREGOR, JOHN, of Delwoxer, with his wife Effie Farquharson, and their youngest son Alexander Grant, in Strathaven, Banffshire, 1708. [NAS.CH1.2.30/1/28]

GRANT, JOHN, in Achelannis, and his wife Effie Gordon, in Strathaven, Banffshire, 1708. [NAS.CH1.2.30/1/28]

GRANT, or GILLIMICHAEL, JOHN, and his wife Margaret Fouler, in Wester Camdel, Strathaven, Banffshire, 1708. [NAS.CH1.2.30/1/28]

GRANT, or MCGILLIMICHAEL, JOHN, and his wife Elisabeth Gib, in Strathaven, Banffshire, 1708. [NAS.CH1.2.30/1/28]

GRANT, JOHN, a student at Douai, 1748. [RSC.I.86]

GRANT, JOHN, of Blairfindy, at Ratisbon Seminary in 1748. [SIG#295][RSC.I.252]

GRANT, JOHN, at Ratisbon Seminary in 1764. [SIG#295][RSC.I.253]

GRANT, KIL., from Strathspey, Morayshire, at Ratisbon Monastery, 1709. [SIG#293]

GRANT, LUDOVICK, at Ratisbon Seminary in 1718. [SIG#294][RSC.I.250]

GRANT, MARGARET, spouse to Donald Grant in Delurogal, Strathaven, Banffshire, 1708. [NAS.CH1.2.30/1/28]

GRANT, MARGARET, in the parish of Bellie, 1710. [NAS.CH1.2.29.3/211]

GRANT, MAURICE, from Strathdon, Aberdeenshire, son of the laird of Auchlichny, at Ratisbon Monastery, 1724. [SIG#293]

GRANT, or MCGREGOR, PATRICK, and his wife Elizabeth......, in Delnabe, Strathaven, Banffshire, 1708. [NAS.CH1.2.30/1/28]

GRANT, PATRICK, in Tomnaraw, Aberdeenshire, 1714. [NLS.ms976.143]

GRANT, PAUL, and family, in Guisachan, Kiltarlity, Inverness-shire, 1710. [NAS.CH1.2.29.3]

GRANT, PETER, in Braemar, Aberdeenshire, 1710. [NAS.CH1.2.29.3]

GRANT, PETER, born 1708 at Blairfindy, son of the laird of Glenfindy, Glenlivet, ordained in Rome 1735, a missionary in Glengarry, Inverness-shire, from 1735 to 1737, returned to Rome in 1737, died there on 1 September 1784. [IR.XVII.51; XVIII.136]

GRANT, ROBERT, at Ratisbon Seminary, 1713. [SIG.294]

GRANT, ROBERT, at Ratisbon Seminary, 1719. [SIG.294][RSC.I.250]

GRANT, ROBERT, at Ratisbon Seminary, 1735. [RSC.I.251]

GRANT, or MCGILLIMICHAEL, WILLIAM, Strathaven, Banffshire, 1708. [NAS.CH1.2.30/1/28]

GRANT, WILLIAM, at the Ratisbon Seminary, 1713. [SIG#294][RSC.I.250]

GRANT, Professor WILLIAM, at the Ratisbon Seminary, 1713. [SIG#294][RSC.I.249]

GRAY, ALEXANDER, servant to James Moor, in Culreach, Parish of Bellie, 1710. [NAS.CH1.2.29.3/211]

GRAY, ANDREW, from Dundee, at the Monastery of Ratisbon from 1641, died in Poland during 1695. [SIG#292]

GRAY, ANDREW, servant to Alexander Tod in Nether Dallachie, in the parish of Bellie, 1710. [NAS.CH1.2.29.3/211]

GRAY, ISOBEL, a servant in Cross, Kinnore parish, 1710. [NAS.CH1.2.29.3/210]

GRAY, JAMES, a servabt in

GRAY, JANET, a servant in Cowie Muir, in the parish of Bellie, 1710. [NAS.CH1.2.29.3/211]

GRAY, JOACHIM, born in Fochabers, Morayshire, in 1715, at Ratisbon Monastery 1739. [SIG#294]

GRAY, MARGARET, life -rentrix of Lumgair, Kincardineshire, 1705. [NAS.CH1.2.5.2]

GRAY, MARGARET, daughter to John Gray a tenant in Nether Achinroth, in the parish of Bellie, 1710. [NAS.CH1.2.29.3/211]

GRAY, MARGARET, in Cottonhill, Parish of Bellie, 1710. [NAS.CH1.2.29.3/211]

GRAY, PETER, a wright in Fochabers, 1710. [NAS.CH1.2.29.3/210]

GRAY, ROBERT, in Fochabers, 1710. [NAS.CH1.2.29.3/210]

GRAY, WILLIAM, a wright in Fochabers, Morayshire, his wife Bessie Achyndachie, sons Peter, John, and Robert, - all wrights, and daughter Isobel, Morayshire, 1705, 1710. [NAS.CH1.2.5/2; 2.29.3/210]

GRAY, ..., relict of Dr Dickson sometime in Montrose, Angus, 1705. [NAS.CH1.2.5.2]

GREEN, JAMES, a tenant in Upper Achinroth, with his wife Marjory Forbes, in the parish of Bellie, 1710. [NAS.CH1.2.29.3/211]

GREEN, PETER, a tenant in Upper Dallachie, Parish of Bellie, 1710. [NAS.CH1.2.29.3/211]

GREGORY, CALLUM, 1714. [NLS.ms976.143]

GRETNA, Lady, a 'papist' In Bull's land, Canongait, 1704. [NAS.CH1.2.5.2/149]

GRIER, MARGARET, in Kirkconnel, Dumfries-shire, widow of John Stewart in New Abbey, 1703. [NAS.CH1.2.5.1]

GRIER, ROBERT, and spouse Janet Laury, with children Agnes, James, John, and Margaret, in Buittle, Kirkcudbrightshire, 1705. [NAS.CH1.2.5.2]

GRIERSON, ALEXANDER, of Dalfad, the younger, with his wife Margaret Cameron, two sons and 2 daughters, in Ardach, in Glenmuick, Tullich, and Glengarden, Aberdeenshire, 1718. [NAS.CH1.2.47/284]

GRIERSON, or MCGRIGOR, CALLUM, of Dalfad, Aberdeenshire, 1714. [NLS.ms976.143]

GRIERSON, DALAN, of Dalfad, and his children Duncan, Calum, and Anne, in Dalfad, in Glenmuick, Tullich, and Glengarden, Aberdeenshire, 1718. [NAS.CH1.2.47/284]

GRIERSON, JAMES, second son of Sir Robert Grierson of Lagg, a student at the Scots College at Douai, 1698; in Carruchen, Troqueer, Dumfries-shire, 1705. [RSC.I.64][NAS.CH1.2.5./3]

GRIERSON, Sir ROBERT, of Lag, an apostate, in Rockall, Mouswald, Dumfries-shire, 1705. [NAS.CH1.2.5/3]

GRIGORY, or MCGRIGOR, CALUM, in Riccary, his wife Elizabeth Tause, and sons John, Duncan, and Calum, Glengarden, Aberdeenshire,1718. [NAS.CH1.2.47.271]

GUTHRIE, Master DAVID, of Carsebank, 'a papist' in Angus, 1704,1705. [NAS.CH1.2.5.3.204; CH1.2.5.2.171]

HACKET, or HALKET ....., a priest in Banffshire, 1710, in the Garioch,1714. [NAS.CH1.2.30/1/5; CH1.2.29.3] [NLS.ms976.143]

HAGGONS, RICHARD, and his wife Isobel Mearns, at the Raws of Huntly, Dunbennan parish, 1710. [NAS.CH1.2.29.3/210]

HAGGS, laird of, Old Monkland parish, 'a papist', 1683. [RPCS.VIII.642]

HAIGHTLIE, MARGARET, a cottar in Buittle, Kirkcudbrightshire, 1705. [NAS.CH1.2.5.2]

HAMILTON, ALEXANDER, at Ratisbon Seminary in 1764. [SIG#295][RSC.I.253]

HAMILTON, JAMES, at Ratisbon Seminary in 1713. [SIG#294][RSC.I.250]

HAMILTON, JAMES, born 1752, at Ratisbon Seminary in 1764. [SIG#295][RSC.I.253]

HAMILTON, MARGARET, spouse to Captain John Wood, a schoolmistress in Edinburgh, 1703. [NAS.CH1.2.5.2/153]

HAMILTON, PLAC., at Ratisbon Seminary in 1709. [SIG#293]

HANNAY, JOHN, his wife Margaret Davidson, and daughters Margaret and Janet, in Dalbeattie, Orr, Dumfries-shire, 1705. [NAS.CH1.2.5/156]

HARRIS, BARBARA, aged 26, in Barnbarrach, Colvend, Dumfries-shire, 1704. [NAS.CH1.2.5.2]

HARRIS, JOHN, a brewer in Cargill, Perthshire, 1704. [NAS.CH1.2.5.3.203]

HARRIS, JOHN, in Achnashein, Colvend, Dumfries-shire, with his wife Janet, and children Barbara (aged 20), John (aged 19), and Janet (aged 14), 1704. [NAS.CH1.2.5.2]

HARRIS, MARGARET, spouse to James Crookshanks, 'a papist' in Linton, 1705. [NAS.CH1.2.5.2.172]

HARRISON, AGNES, in Fochabers, Morayshire, 1705. [NAS.CH1.2.5/2]

HARRISON, ANNE, servant to the Marquess of Huntly, parish of Bellie, 1710. [NAS.CH1.2.29.3]

HARRISON, WILLIAM, born near Elgin, ordained in Rome during 1737, priest in Morar, Knoydart, Arisaig and Keppoch, died in Keppoch during 1773. [IR.XVIII.138]

HAY, AGNES, wife to John Geddes tenant in Upper Achinroth, in the parish of Bellie, 1710. [NAS.CH1.2.29.3/211]

HAY, ALEXANDER, tenant in Nether Dallachie, and his wife Margaret Geddes, in the parish of Bellie, 1710. [NAS.CH1.2.29.3/211]

HAY, BENEDICT, of Dalgetty, from Wurzburg to Ratisbon in 1673. [SF#280]

HAY, GEORGE, a priest in Aberlour, Morayshire, 1710. [NAS.CH1.2.30/1/5]

HAY, GEORGE, bishop of Edinburgh, 1781. [NAS.GD44.43.253]

HAY, ISOBEL, daughter of the late John Hay, ground laborer, and his wife Margaret Fraser , who was baptised as a Protestant when an infant, was baptised by on 29 September 1697 by Father Robert Francis. [SNQ.VIII.182]

HAY, ISOBEL, in Fochabers, Morayshire, 1705. [NAS.CH1.2.5/2]

HAY, JAMES, from Stobhall, diocese of Dunkeld, educated at the Scots College in Paris from 1777 to 1782. [SCP#218]

HAY, JOHN, servant to a gardener in Fetteresso, Kincardineshire, 1704. [NAS.CH1.2.5.3/201]

HAY, JOHN, a shoemaker in Fochabers, Morayshire, 1705, 1710.
[NAS.CH1.2.5/2; 2.29.3/210]

HAY, JOHN, a footman at Gordon Castle, Morayshire, 1705. [NAS.CH1.2.5/187]

HAY, JOHN, a workman in Fochabers, his wife Helen Gairn or Garden, and children John and Marjorie Hay, Morayshire, 1705. [NAS.CH1.2.5/2]

HAY, MARJORIE, daughter of William Hay, a merchant burgess of Aberdeen, and his wife Anna Gordon, Protestants, who was baptised as a Protestant when an infant, was baptised by on 29 September 1697 by Father Robert Francis. [SNQ.VIII.182]

HAY, MARJORY, Parish of Bellie, 1710. [NAS.CH1.2.29.3/211]

HAY, PETER, educated at the Scots College in Paris around 1770, ordained in Paris 1777, died in Auchinhalrig, 17 December 1783. [SCP#218]

HAY, WILLIAM, brother of the Earl of Kinnoull, a student at the Scots College at Douai, 1685. [RSC.I.57]

HAY, WILLIAM, in Perth, 1782. [IR.XVII.77]

HENDERSON, JOHN, at Ratisbon Seminary, 1719. [SIG#294][RSC.I.251]

HENDERSON, MARGARET, 'an aged woman', in the Cotterton of Achintowell, Aberchirder, 1710. [NAS.CH1.2.29.3]

HENRY, JEAN, mother of Robert Corson, in New Abbey, Dumfries-shire, 1703. [NAS.CH1.2.5.1]

HENRY, JOSEPH, a student at the Scots College at Valladolid, 1774. [RSC.I.206]

HEPBURN, ANNA, relict of ...... Fyffe, in Con's Close, Edinburgh, 'a papist' in Old Kirk parish, Edinburgh, 1704/1705. [NAS.CH1.2.5.2.149;175/1]

HEPBURN, Major JAMES, and his daughter Margaret Hepburn, at Fochabers Milne, Morayshire, 1705. [NAS.CH1.2.5/187]

HERRIES, JAMES, of Glaister, in Terregles and Kirkgunzeon, Dumfries-shire, 1705. [NAS.CH1.2.5.2]

HERRIES, JAMES, born 1753, son of Robert Herries of Auchenshun and Joan Douglas, a student at Douai, 1764. [RSC.I.92]

HERRIES, JOHN, son of John Herries of Auchencheen and Elizabeth Gordon, a student at the Scots College in Madrid, 1734. [RSC.I.200]

HERRIES, KATHERINE, widow of bailie Romer, in Dumfries, 1704. [NAS.CH1.2.5.2]

HERRIES, KATHERINE, relict of John Roome late bailie of Dumfries, 1705. [NAS.CH1.2.5.1]

HERRIES, KILLIAN, born 1663, at Ratisbon Monastery 1679, died 1683. [SF#280]

HERRIES, MARY, in Terregles, Dumfries-shire, 1703. [NAS.CH1.2.5.1]

HERRIES, ROBERT, son of John Herries of Auchencheen, Minihive, and Elizabeth Gordon, a student at the Scots College in Madrid, 1722. [RSC.I.200]

HERRIS, MARION, servant to Robert Brown of Bishopton, Kirkmahoe, Dumfries-shire, 1704. [NAS.CH1.52.2]

HISLOP, JAMES, in Cowand, in Terregles and Kirkgunzeon, Dumfries-shire, 1705. [NAS.CH1.2.5.2]

HOME, JANET, spouse to William Abercromby an Episcopal minister, in Edinburgh, 'a papist' living in Forrester's Wynd, New North Kirk parish, Edinburgh, 1704/1705. [NAS.CH1.2.5.2.149/154;175/1]

HOPKINS, MARY, relict of Robert McBrair a messenger in Dumfries, 1705. [NAS.CH1.2.5.1]

HORN, ALEXANDER, born 1762, at Ratisbon Seminary, 1772. [SIG#295][RSC.I.253]

HORN, ELSPETH, in Fochabers, Morayshire, 1705. [NAS.CH1.2.5/2]

HORN, MARY, servant in Fochabers, Morayshire, 1705. [NAS.CH1.2.5/2,187]

HOSSACK, ANDREW, in Morayshire, 1705. [NAS.CH1.2.5/2]

HOSSACK, ANDREW, a weaver in Keith, Banffshire, 1794. [NAS.SC2.72.4]

HOSSACK, GEORGE, a weaver in Morayshire, 1705. [NAS.CH1.2.5/2]

HOSSACK, GEORGE, a weaver, with his children Andrew and Marjory, Parish of Bellie, 1710. [NAS.CH1.2.29.3/211]

HOSSACK, JANET, in Fochabers, 1710. [NAS.CH1.2.29.3/210]

HUGO, MARGARET, in Strageth, Auchterarder, Perthshire, 1703. [NAS.CH1.2.5.2]

HUME, ANNA, gentlewoman to Lady Kilsyth, in Glasgow, 1703, 1705. [NAS.CH1.2.5.1/3]

HUME, JOHN, servant to the laird of Niddrie, an apostate and a 'papist' in Liberton, Edinburgh, 1704. [NAS.CH1.2.5.2.149]

HUNTLY, Earl of, at Gordon Castle, Morayshire, 1705. [NAS.CH1.2.5/187]

HUNTER, ISOBEL, aged over 70 years, relict of James Semple, at Castle Semple, Renfrewshire, 1704. [NAS.CH1.2.5.3.202]

HUNTER, LEONARD, in Cannonmills, a 'papist', his wife Margaret Allan, a Protestant, and their daughter, in West Kirk parish, Edinburgh, 1704. [NAS.CH1.2.5.2.149]

HUNTER, LEONARD, in West Kirk parish, Edinburgh, 1703. [NAS.CH1.2.5.2/151]

HUTCHEON, JEAN, in Fochabers, Morayshire, 1705; a servant in Fochabers, 1710. [NAS.CH1.2.5/2; 2.29.3/210]

HUTCHEON, MARGARET, in Fochabers, Morayshire, and her children Margaret and Jean Donald, 1705; teacher at a girls school in Fochabers, 1710. [NAS.CH1.2.5/2,187; 29.3/210]

HUTTON, AGNES, servant to Robert Brown of Bishopton, Kirkmahoe, Dumfries, 1705. [NAS.CH1.2.5.1]

HUTTON, BARBARA, in Mabie, in Traquair, Dumfries-shire, 1703. [NAS.CH1.2.5.1]

IMLACH, ALEXANDER, a tanner in Fochabers, Morayshire, his wife Agnes Coutts, and daughters Agnes and Elisabeth, 1705. [NAS.CH1.2.5/2]

IMLACH, ALEXANDER, a shoemaker, and his daughters Isabel and Elspet, in Fochabers, 1710. [NAS.CH1.2.29.3/210]

INGLIS, ISOBEL, servant to Alexander Tod in Nether Dallachie, in the parish of Bellie, 1710. [NAS.CH1.2.29.3/211]

INGLIS, JOHN, and his wife Isobel Leith, in Fochabers, 1710. [NAS.CH1.2.29.3/210]

INGLIS, WILLIAM, a student at the Scots College at Douai, 1685. [RSC.I.57]

INNES, ADAM, in Germans, Athelstaneford, East Lothian, with his four children, 1703. [NAS.CH1.2.5.1]

INNES, ALEXANDER, in Muldorie, Morayshire, 1705. [NAS.CH1.2.5/2]

INNES, ALEXANDER, a tenant, and his wife Bessie Gordon, also sons Alexander and William, in Fochabers, 1710. [NAS.CH1.2.29.3/210]

INNES, CHARLES, in Drumgask, his spouse Claudia Irving, Aboyne or Glentanar, Aberdeenshire, 1704. [NAS.CH1.2.5/190]

INNES, CHARLES, master of the house to the Marquess of Huntly, parish of Bellie, 1710. [NAS.CH1.2.29.3]

INNES, CHARLES, son of James Innes of Balnacraig and Catherine Gordon, a student at Douai, 1749. [RSC.I.87]

INNES, FRANCIS, a merchant in Aberdeen, 1705, 1714. [NAS.CH1.2.5.2/155] [NLS.ms976.143]

INNES, GEORGE, born July 1683, son of Charles Innes and Claudia Irvine, educated at the Scots College in Paris, ordained in Paris in 1712, a priest at Morar in 1714, later in Scallan, Glenlivet, Banffshire, 1717-1721, at the Scots College in Paris from 1727 until his death on 29 April 1752. [NLS.ms68, fos.31-32][SCP#212]

INNES, GEORGE, son of Innes of Drumgask, 1714. [NLS.ms976.143]

INNES, HENRY, born at Ballogie in 1748, son of James Innes, educated at the Scots College in Paris 1759, ordained in 1771, died at Ballogie on 11 November 1833. [SCP#218]

INNES, ISOBELL, Lady Easter Dunoon, 'a papist' in Angus, 1705. [NAS.CH1.2.5.2.171]

INNES, JOHN, born 31 July 1668, son of James Innes of Drumgask, a student at the Scots College at Douai, 1681; a Jesuit priest in Glengarden, Aberdeenshire, 1714, 1718. [RSC.I.58][NLS.ms976.143][NAS.CH1.2.47.271]

INNES, LEWIS, son of Francis Innes, master of the Aberdeen Shore-works, and his wife Jean Maitland, was baptised by John ..... a Jesuit, in Aberdeen on 20 June 1688, godfather was Lewis Innes, Principal of the Scots College in Paris, and was educated at the Scots College in Paris from 1704 to 1709. [SNQ.VIII.181][SCP#214]

INNES, LEWIS, son of James Innes, nephew of Principal George Innes in the diocese of Aberdeen, educated at the Scots College in Paris 1741, father of William Innes a priest. [SCP#217]

INNES, LIZIE, in the parish of Bellie, 1710. [NAS.CH1.2.29.3/211]

INNES, ROBERT, born 27 April 1690, son of Francis Innes and his wife Jean Maitland in St Nicolas parish, Aberdeen, was baptised on 27 April 1690 by Father Robert Francis, godfather was William Gordon a merchant in Aberdeen, and godmother was Henrietta Gordon wife of James Panton in Aberdeen. [SNQ.VIII.181]

INNES, ROBERT, rector of the Scots College at Douai, 1752. [RSC.I.89]

INNES, WALTER, in Fochabers, 1710. [NAS.CH1.2.29.3/210]

INNES, WALTER, formerly prior of a convent in Burgundy, later in Drumgask, 1714.[NLS.ms976.143]

IRVIN, ALEXANDER, born 1666, son of Richard Irvin of Carnfield and Margaret Oliphant, a student at the Scots College at Douai, 1681. [RSC.I.56]

IRVINE, AGNES, wife of John Morison in Kirkconnel, New Abbey, Dumfries-shire, 1703. [NAS.CH1.2.5.1]

IRVINE, FRANCIS, of Hiltoun, 1690. [RPCS.XV.99]

IRVINE, JAMES MARIANUS, possibly of Belty, Abbot of Wurzburg 1685 to his death in 1688. [SF#280]

IRVINE, MARIE, born 1626, daughter of a Catholic nobleman who fled to France, moved to Canada in 1642, then in Dieppe, France, from 1643 to 1657, returned to Canada as a nun in 1657, entered the Hotel Dieu, died in Quebec on 14 November 1687. [DCB]

IRVINE, MARY, spouse to James Smith formerly a gardener to the Earl of Nithsdale, in Terregles, Dumfries-shire, 1703. [NAS.CH1.2.5.1]

IRVINE, PATRICK, born 1627, late of Bealty, Kincardineshire, 1705. [NAS.CH1.2.5.2]

IRVINE, WILLIAM, in Bowhouse, Terregles, Dumfries-shire, 1703. [NAS.CH1.2.5.1]

IRVING, AGNES, in Troquair, Orr, Dumfries-shire, 1705. [NAS.CH1.2.5/156]

IRVING, JAMES, a cottar in Mabie, Troquair, Orr, Dumfries-shire, 1703,1705. [NAS.CH1.2.5.1/156]

IRVING, JANET, Lady Terraughtie, and her children Alexander Maxwell, Halbert Maxwell, Lucy Maxwell, Rachel Maxwell, and William Maxwell, in Traquair, Dumfries-shire, 1703. [NAS.CH1.2.5.1]

IRVING, JANET, and her son William Maxwell, in Troquair, Orr, Dumfries-shire, 1705. [NAS.CH1.2.5/156]

IRVING, MARION, in Troquair, Orr, Dumfries-shire, 1705. [NAS.CH1.2.5/156]

IRVING, WILLIAM, a groom in Terregles and Kirkgunzeon, Dumfries-shire, 1705. [NAS.CH1.2.5.2]

IRWING, ..., a priest in Bellie, Banffshire, 1710. [NAS.CH1.2.30/1/5]

JAMIESON, JOHN, in Fochabers, 1710. [NAS.CH1.2.29.3/210]

JAMIESON, JOHN, an alleged priest who had returned to Scotland was imprisoned in Aberdeen Tolbooth in 1690. [RPCS.XVI.469]

JAMIESON, MARGARET, daughter of the late John Jamieson, a Protestant and a merchant of Aberdeen, and his deceased wife Jean Blackburn, a Catholic, in the parish of St Nicolas, Aberdeen, was baptised as a Protestant when an infant, later baptised by Father Robert Francis on 29 September 1696. [SNQ.VIII.181]

JESSIMAN, AGNES, spouse to John Forbes in Brownhill, Glass, 1710. [NAS.CH1.2.29.3]

JESSIMAN, ISOBEL, in Gibstoun, Kinnoir parish, 1710. [NAS.CH1.2.29.3/210]

JESSIMAN, JAMES, at the Raws of Huntly, Dunbennan parish, 1710. [NAS.CH1.2.29.3/210]

JESSIMAN, MARGARET, at the Raws of Huntly, Dunbennan parish, 1710. [NAS.CH1.2.29.3/210]

JESSIMAN, WILLIAM, at the Raws of Huntly, Dunbennan parish, 1710. [NAS.CH1.2.29.3/210]

JOHNSTON, AGNES, wife to John Chapman, in Cowie Muir, in the parish of Bellie, 1710. [NAS.CH1.2.29.3/211]

JOHNSTON, ANDREW, a subtenant in Cumry, and his wife Bessie Duncan, also daughter Helen Johnston, in Ruthven, Strathbogie,1710. [NAS.CH1.2.29.3/209]

JOHNSTON, ANNA, daughter of John Johnston a weaver in Robslaw, Aberdeen, was baptised by Father Robert Francis on 29 September 1696. [SNQ.VIII.181]

JOHNSTON, ANNA, servant to Dame Anna Douglas in Collinton, Edinburgh, 1703. [NAS.CH1.2.5.2/151]

JOHNSTON, GEORGE, in Robestoun, Kinnoir parish, 1710. [NAS.CH1.2.29.3/210]

JOHNSTON, ISOBEL, in Ruthven, Strathbogie,1710. [NAS.CH1.2.29.3/209]

JOHNSTON, ISOBEL, a servant in Nether Dallachie, in the parish of Bellie, 1710. [NAS.CH1.2.29.3/211]

JOHNSTON, JAMES, a student at Douai, 1750. [RSC.I.87]

JOHNSTONE, JEAN, relict of .... Johnstone son of the deceased Robert Johnstone late town major, with three children Jean, Helen, and ...., 'a papist' in Ferrier's land, College Kirk parish, Edinburgh, 1703/1704/1705. [NAS.CH1.2.5.2.149/151;175/1]

JOHNSTON, JEAN, servant in Lomond, Kinnoir parish, 1710. [NAS.CH1.2.29.3/210]

JOHNSTON, JOHN, of Clanthery, Closeburn, Dumfries-shire, 1705. [NAS.CH1.2.5.1]

JOHNSTON, MARGARET, relict of .... Ker, an apostate, in Hart's Close, College Kirk parish, Edinburgh, 1703. [NAS.CH1.2.5.2/151]

JOHNSTON, MARGARET, in Landends, Parish of Bellie, 1710. [NAS.CH1.2.29.3/211]

JOHNSTON, PETER, in Ruthven, Strathbogie,1710. [NAS.CH1.2.29.3/209]

JOHNSTONE, ..., relict of William Home a merchant burgess of Glasgow, alias Mrs Ker who lives in Hart's Close, 'a papist' in Heart's Close, College Kirk parish, Edinburgh, 1704/1705. [NAS.CH1.2.5.2.149;175/1]

JOHNSTON, ..., a priest in Angus, 1704. [NAS.CH1.2.5/204]

JOHNSTON, Mrs, gentlewoman to Lady Stewart in College Kirk parish, Edinburgh, 1703. [NAS.CH1.2.5.2/151]

KAIMS, EDWARD, in Barnbarrach, Colvend, Dumfries, 1704. [NAS.CH1.2.5.2]

KEIR, ALEXANDER, with his sister Rebeka, in Ardach, in Glenmuick, Tullich, and Glengarden, Aberdeenshire, 1718. [NAS.CH1.2.47/284]

KEIR, CALUM, with his wife Isabel Coutts and two children, in Lairy, in Glenmuick, Tullich, and Glengarden, Aberdeenshire, 1718. [NAS.CH1.2.47/284]

KEIR, DUNCAN, of Stranettan, with his wife, two sons and two daughters in Forme(?),in Glenmuick, Tullich, and Glengarden, Aberdeenshire, 1718. [NAS.CH1.2.47/284]

KEIR, JAMES, his wife Janet Glass, and 1 child in Riahloin, 1718. [NAS.CH1.2.7.271]

KEIR, JAMES, in Strainlea, with his wife Moira Michie, two sons and one daughter, in Forme(?),in Glenmuick, Tullich, and Glengarden, Aberdeenshire,1718. [NAS.CH1.2.47/284]

KEIR, JANET, a widow, with her son Calum Cameron and his two children, in Ardach, in Glenmuick, Tullich, and Glengarden, Aberdeenshire, 1718. [NAS.CH1.2.47/284]

KEIR, JANET, wife of John Forbes, in Ardach, in Glenmuick, Tullich, and Glengarden, Aberdeenshire, 1718. [NAS.CH1.2.47/284]

KEIR, THOMAS, a servant in Riahloin, 1718. [NAS.CH1.2.7.271]

KEITH, Lady MARY, aged 10 years, daughter of the Earl Marischal, a papist residing in Mrs Jean Drummond's house in Taylor's land, Canongait, 1703/1704. [NAS.CH1.2.5.2/149/151]

KEITH, ..., a priest in Banffshire, 1710. [NAS.CH1.2.30/1/5]

KELMAN, MARGARET, in Easterton of Arbrek, Botriphnie, 1710. [NAS.CH1.2.29.3]

KEMMIE, ELSPET, wife to James Cuie a tenant in Cottonhill, Parish of Bellie, 1710. [NAS.CH1.2.29.3/211]

KEMMIE, MARJORY, wife of Andrew Hossack, and her daughter Anne Nicol, parish of Bellie, 1710. [NAS.CH1.2.29.3]

KEMPT, ELSPET, in Cottonhill, 'frequents popish meetings', Parish of Bellie, 1710. [NAS.CH1.2.29.3/211]

KEMP, JANET, servant in Fochabers, Morayshire, 1705. [NAS.CH1.2.5/2, 187]

KEMPT, MARGARET, a servant at Burnside, parish of Bellie, 1710. [NAS.CH1.2.29.3]

KEMPT, ROBERT, tenant in Cottonhill, with his wife Catherine Bremner, and son William, Parish of Bellie, 1710. [NAS.CH1.2.29.3/211]

KENDALL, ELIZABETH, gentlewoman to the Duchess of Gordon, in Canongait, 1703. [NAS.CH1.2.5.2/151]

KENDALL, SUSANNA, 'a papist' in Canongait, Edinburgh, 1705. [NAS.CH1.2.5.2.170]

KENNAN, BARBARA, spouse to Robert Howat or Herris a merchant at Bridgend, and son John, in Troquair, Orr, Dumfries-shire, 1705; 'a papist' in Linton, 1705. [NAS.CH1.2.5.2.156/172]

KENNAN, JOHN, servant to John Kennan in Troquair, Orr, Dumfries-shire, 1703. [NAS.CH1.2.5.1]

KENNAN, JOHN, 'a papist' in Linton, 1705. [NAS.CH1.2.5.2.172]

KENNAN, JOHN, with his sons John, Joseph, Lucy, and Mary, in Cargan, Troquair, Orr, Dumfries-shire, 1703/1705. [NAS.CH1.2.5.1/156]

KENNEDY, ALEXANDER, a blind fiddler in Kilchassie, Atholl, Perthshire, 1705. [NAS.CH1.2.5.2.165]

KENNEDY, ALEXANDER, from the Diocese of Dunkeld, ordained at Scalan around 1767, priest in Arisaig and the Small Isles, died in Arisaig on 11 July 1773. [IR.XVIII.148]

KENNEDY, BEATRIX, spouse to George Stevenson son of Dr Stevenson in Edinburgh, 'papists' in West Kirk parish, Edinburgh, 1704. [NAS.CH1.2.5.2.149]

KENNEDY, ELIZABETH, spouse to James Stevenson, son of Dr Stevenson, in Collington, Edinburgh, 1703. [NAS.CH1.2.5.2/151]

KENNEDY, ILDEPHONSUS, at Ratisbon Monastery in 1742. [SIG#294]

KENNEDY, JOHN, gardener to Lord Drummond, with his wife Mary Lader and his children Lilias, Mary, and Thomas, in Auchterarder, Perthshire, 1703. [NAS.CH1.2.5.2]

KENNEDY, THOMAS, at Ratisbon Monastery in 1719. [SIG#294]

KENNEDY, THOMAS, at Ratisbon Monastery in 1735. [RSC.I.251]

KERMONT, MARY, spouse to John Taylor a gardener in Fochabers, Morayshire, and their daughter Jean Taylor, 1705. [NAS.CH1.2.5/187]

KERR, Lady GRADDIN, with her children Jean Kerr aged 18,Henry Kerr, Alexander Kerr aged 11,Lilias Kerr, Archibald Kerr, James Kerr, and Helen Kerr aged 8, in Old Kirk parish Edinburgh, 1703, then in Leith, 'papists' in Broad Wynd, South Leith, Edinburgh, 1704/1705. [NAS.CH1.2.5.2.149/151/170]

KIMBER, JANET, in Nether Dallachie, in the parish of Bellie, 1710. [NAS.CH1.2.29.3/211]

KING, SICILIE, Parish of Bellie, 1710. [NAS.CH1.2.29.3/211]

KINNAIRD, ELIZABETH, spouse to Charles Ritchie, 'himself being abroad', in Tron Kirk parish, Edinburgh, 1703. [NAS.CH1.2.5.2/151]

KNIGHT, JOHN, a servant to Norman Hutcheson an officer in Fochabers, Morayshire, 1705. [NAS.CH1.2.5/2, 187]

KNIGHT, JOHN, a weaver, with his wife Barbara Umphrey, and children Janet and John, in Fochabers, 1710. [NAS.CH1.2.29.3/210]

KOBAN, MARGARET, daughter to Helen Gordon, in Bettie,1710. [NAS.CH1.2.9.3]

KYD, FRANCES, servant to Lady Mary Keith, a 'papist' residing in Mrs Jean Drummond's house, Taylor's land, Canongait, 1704. [NAS.CH1.2.5.2/149]

LAHASSIE, PETER, a Frenchman who has a dancing school, and Isobel Abercromby, his spouse, ' papists' in Tron Kirk parish, later in New Kirk parish, Edinburgh, 1704/1705. [NAS.CH1.2.5.2.149;175/1]

LAING, AGNES, spouse to Francis Steel in Charleston, Aboyne or Glentanar, Aberdeenshire, 1704. [NAS.CH1.2.5/190]

LAMB, JOHN, a tailor on the South Water of Leith, his wife Beatrix Henderson, a school teacher, and their 20 year old daughter Mary Lamb, apostates and 'papists' in West Kirk parish, Edinburgh, 1704. [NAS.CH1.2.5.2.149/153]

LARGO, Lady, an apostate, 'a papist' in the Abbey, Canongait parish, Edinburgh, 1703/1704/1705. [NAS.CH1.2.5.2.149/151/170]

LATIMER, JANET, in Troquair, Orr, Dumfries-shire, 1705. [NAS.CH1.2.5/156]

LAURIE, JAMES, a tenant or cottar in Mabie, with his spouse Agnes Carlyle, in Traquair, Dumfries-shire, 1703. [NAS.CH1.2.5.1]

LAUSON, WILLIAM, a 'papist' and an apostate, with his wife, in Liberton, Edinburgh, 1704. [NAS.CH1.2.5.2.149/154]

LAWPER, JANET, in Robestoun, Kinnoir parish, 1710. [NAS.CH1.2.29.3/210]

LEARMONT, JOHN, servant to William Lindsay of Wachop, Colvend, Dumfries-shire, 1704. [NAS.CH1.2.5.2]

LEITH, ALEXANDER, in Oldnoth, Rhynie, with his wife Barbara Gordon and young children, 1710. [NAS.CH1.2.29.3/209]

LEITH, GEORGE, at Ratisbon Seminary, 1718. [SIG#294][RSC.I.250]

LEITH, Mrs JEAN, in Edinburgh, 'a papist' lodging with Mr John Riddoch, Old Kirk parish, Edinburgh, 1704/1705. [NAS.CH1.2.5.2.149/175/1]

LEITH, JOHN, a brewer in Gallowtoun, Byfoot, 'a papist' in Fife, 1705. [NAS.CH1.2.5.2.174/2]

LEITH, JOHN, son of Antony Leith and ..... Forbes, a student at Douai, 1749. [RSC.I.87]

LEITH, Mrs MARGARET, in Edinburgh, 'a papist' lodging with John Riddoch in Old Kirk parish, then in Tron Kirk parish, Edinburgh, 1704/1705. [NAS.CH1.2.5.2.149;175/1]

LEITH, ROBERT, at Ratisbon Seminary, 1718. [SIG#294]

LEITH, ..., son of Alexander Leith in Collithy, at Ratisbon Seminary, 1726. [SIG#294]

LESLIE, BONIFACE, son of Alexander Leslie of Pitcaple, at Ratisbon Monastery in 1709. [SIG#293]

LESLIE, ERNEST, son of Charles Leslie and Elizabeth Fordyce, a student at the Scots College in Madrid, 1722. [RSC.I.200]

LESLIE, ERNEST, born 1776, son of John Leslie of Balquhain, at Ratisbon Seminary, 1788. [SIG#295][RSC.I.254]

LESLIE, JANET, wife to James Chapman, and her children, Alexander, Isobel, and Janet, 'frequents the popish meetings', Parish of Bellie, 1710. [NAS.CH1.2.29.3/211]

LESLIE, JAMES, son of Alexander Leslie of Pitcaple, a student at the Scots College at Douai, 1695. [RSC.I.63]

LESLIE, JAMES, 'sister son' to Alexander Gordon of Camrie, was sent abroad for education in 1719. [NLS.ms68.31-32]; ordained in Rome in 1729, a priest in Uist, Morar, and Arasaig, moved to France after 1745, died in Courtrai in 1780. [IR.XVIII.134]

LESLIE, JOHN, at Ratisbon Seminary 1713, died 1779. [SIG#294][RSC.I.250]

LESLIE, JOHN, born 1781, son of John Leslie of Balquhain, at Ratisbon Seminary in 1788. [SIG#295][RSC.I.254]

LESLIE, WALTER, of Pitcaple, a student at the Scots College at Douai, 1682. [RSC.I.57]

LESLIE, ..., of Balquhain, at Fetternear, Fordyce, 1714. [NLS.ms976.143]

LEWARS, JOHN, the elder in Townhead of Kirkconnel, Dumfries-shire, 1703. [NAS.CH1.2.5.1]

LEWARS, ROBERT, a tenant of the laird of Shambillie, and his wife Agnes Carruthers, sons Andrew aged 13, and Herbert, in New Abbey, Dumfries-shire, 1703. [NAS.CH1.2.5.1]

LEWARS, ROBERT, tenant to the laird of Shambillie, and his daughter Jean aged 12, in New Abbey, Dumfries-shire, 1703. [NAS.CH1.2.5.1]

LINDSAY, CONSTANCE, in Colvend, Dumfries-shire, 1704. [NAS.CH1.2.5.2]

LINDSAY, ELIZABETH, relict of the late Robert Kirk wadsetter of Lochdougan, in Kelton, Kirkcudbrightshire, 1705. [NAS.CH1.2.5.2]

LINDSAY, WILLIAM, in Colvend, Dumfries-shire, 1704. [NAS.CH1.2.5.2]

LITHGOW, JANET, in Canongait, Edinburgh, 1703. [NAS.CH1.2.5.2/151]

LIVERANCE, WILLIAM, a boy in the house of James Paterson in Edinburgh, 1703. [NAS.CH1.2.5.2]

LIVINGSTONE, MARGARET, in Fochabers, Morayshire, 1705; wife to Robert Hay, in Fochabers, 1710. [NAS.CH1.2.5/2; 2.29.3/210]

LOBBAN, ADAM, a tenant, with his wife Isobel Shand, Parish of Bellie, 1710. [NAS.CH1.2.29.3/211]

LOBBAN, ISOBEL, a servant, late from Ruthven, now in Rothiemay, Strathbogie, 1710. [NAS.CH1.2.29.3]

LOBBAN, JEAN, wife of Alexander Simson, in Fochabers, 1710. [NAS.CH1.2.29.3/210]

LOBBAN, MARY, wife to Andrew Robertson, in Bogmuir in the parish of Bellie, 1710. [NAS.CH1.2.29.3/211]

LOBBAN, WILLIAM, a servant in Fochabers, Morayshire, 1705. [NAS.CH1.2.5/2, 187]

LOGAN, ISOBEL, a 'papist' in Liberton, Edinburgh, 1704. [NAS.CH1.2.5.2.149]

LOGAN, JOHN, a servant in Mabie, Orr, Dumfries-shire, 1703. [NAS.CH1.2.5.1]

LORIMER, ISABEL, in Lochrutton, Dumfries-shire, 1703. [NAS.CH1.2.5.1]

LORIMER, JANET, the younger, a tenant or cottar in Cargan, Traquair, Dumfries-shire, 1703. [NAS.CH1.2.5.1]

LORIMER, JANET, the elder, a tenant or cottar in Cargan, Traquair, Dumfries-shire, 1703. [NAS.CH1.2.5.1]

LORIMER, JOHN, herd to the laird of Kirkconnel, and son James aged 12, in New Abbey, Dumfries-shire, 1703. [NAS.CH1.2.5.1]

LUKE, JOHN, a subtenant in Cumry, and his wife Janet Sivwright, in Ruthven, Strathbogie,1710. [NAS.CH1.2.29.3/209]

LURBIE or LUCKIE, ALEXANDER, a tailor in Huntland Bush, Cargill, Perthshire, with his wife Marjorie McGill, and two children; 1704. [NAS.CH1.2.5.3.203]

MCALISTER, or MACDONELL, RONALD, in Glengarry, Inverness-shire, 1703.

MCALLISTER, DONALD, with his wife Mary More, and son John, apostates in Comar, Kiltarlity, 1679. [IR.XXIV.82]

MCALLISTER, RODERICK, and his wife Elspet Chleirich, apostates in Comar, Kiltarlity, 1679. [IR.XXIV.82]

MCANDREW, DONALD, with his wife, two sons, and two daughters, in Ardach, in Glenmuick, Tullich, and Glengarden, Aberdeenshire, 1718. [NAS.CH1.2.47/284]

MCANDREW, ISOBEL, a widow, with her son William Alanach, in Lairy, in Glenmuick, Tullich, and Glengarden, Aberdeenshire, 1718. [NAS.CH1.2.47/284]

MCANDREW, JAMES, with his wife Margery Keir, and three children, in Lairy, in Glenmuick, Tullich, and Glengarden, Aberdeenshire,1718. [NAS.CH1.2.47/284]

MCANDREW, JANET, a widow, with one daughter, in Lairy, in Glenmuick, Tullich, and Glengarden, Aberdeenshire, 1718. [NAS.CH1.2.47/284]

MCANDREW, JOHN, 'excommunicated for apostacy', with his wife Margaret Keir and two children, in Lairy, in Glenmuick, Tullich, and Glengarden, Aberdeenshire, 1718. [NAS.CH1.2.47/284]

MCANDREW, WILLIAM, at the Raws of Huntly, Dunbennan parish, 1710. [NAS.CH1.2.29.3/210]

MCANGUS, DUNCAN (?), with his wife Janet Forbes,and daughter Janet, in Lairy, in Glenmuick, Tullich, and Glengarden, Aberdeenshire, 1718. [NAS.CH1.2.47/284]

MCARTHUR, ALLAN, born on Canna 1767, emigrated to Cape Breton Island in 1827, died at Sydney Mines on 18 May 1869. [McArthur Cemetery, C.B.]

MCCARTNEY, CHARLES, and his wife Barbara Maxwell aged 24, daughter of John Maxwell of Slayman, in Kelton, Kirkcudbrightshire, 1705. [NAS.CH1.2.5.2]

MACCHANDICH, NIEL, in Eigg, Inverness-shire, 1703. [NAS.CH1.2.5.2]

MCCOIL, DONALD, with his family of six, in Kirkton of Comar, Kiltarlity, Inverness-shire, 1710. [NAS.CH1.2.29.3]

MCCOIL, NIEL, in Morar, Inverness-shire, 1703. [NAS.CH1.2.5.2]

MCCOILDOWIE, JOHN, in Guisachan, Kiltarlity, Inverness-shire, 1710. [NAS.CH1.2.29.3]

MCCOIL........, ALEXANDER, and family, in Kirkton of Comar, Kiltarlity, Inverness-shire, 1710. [NAS.CH1.2.29.3]

MCCONCHIE, DUGAL, in Breacharnoy, Glengarry, Morar, Inverness-shire,1703. [NAS.CH1.2.5.2]

MCCORNOCK, MARY, daughter of the late Charles McCornock and Elizabeth Martine in Edinburgh, 1703. [NAS.CH1.2.5.2]

MCCORNOCK, ..., a widow, 'a papist' in Canongait, Edinburgh, 1705. [NAS.CH1.2.5.2.170]

MCCRAW, ALEXANDER, a priest in Kilmorack, 1714, in Strathglass or Glenmoriston, 1720. [NLS.ms976.143] [NLS.ms68.31-32]

MCCRAE, CHRISTOPHER, chamberlain to the laird of Comer, Inverness-shire, 1703. [NAS.CH1.2.5.2]

MCDONALD, ALEXANDER, in Trotternish, Skye, chamberlain to Sir Donald McDonald of Sleat, 1703. [NAS.CH1.2.5.2]

MCDONALD, ALEXANDER, with children – Donald, Alexander, Mary, Una, Margaret, Katherine (born 1700), and John (born 1701), in Flodigeary, Kilmory, Trotternish, Skye, 1703. [NAS.CH1.2.5.2]

MCDONALD, ALEXANDER, tenant of Aberarder on the forfeited estate of Cluny, was 'turned out as a papist' in 1726. [NAS.GD44.27.10]

MACDONALD, ALEXANDER, of Kinlochmoidart, born 1719, ordained in Rome possibly in 1746, priest in Knoydart until 1773 then in Keppoch, died there on 13 March 1797. [IR.XVIII.141]

MACDONALD, ALEXANDER, born 1725, son of Ranald MacDonald of Scotus, ordained in Rome, priest in Uist, died in Edinburgh during 1756. [IR.XVIII.144]

MCDONALD, ALEXANDER, 1755. [NAS.HCR.I.89]

MACDONALD, ALEXANDER, son of the laird of Bornish, South Uist, ordained in Rome during 1765, priest in Barra until 1780 when he was consecrated a bishop, died 12 September 1791 at Salamanan. [IR.XVIII.147]

MCDONALD, ALEXANDER, Bishop, tack of Samalaman in Moydart, 1786. [NAS.GD201/5/1190]

MACDONALD, ALEXANDER, of Scotus, ordained in Rome by 1767, priest in Knoydart and at Scotus, led emigrants to Canada, founded St Raphael [Charlottenburg] parish, Glengarry, died there in 1803. [IR.XVIII.148]

MACDONALD, ALEXANDER, ordained at Douai in 1775, priest in Uist until 1781, died in Wurzburg, Germany, on 2 January 1810. [IR.XVIII. 152]

MACDONALD, ALEXANDER, born in Clianaig, Glen Spean, in December 1753, son of Archibald MacDonald, educated at the Scots College in Paris 1767, ordained in Valladolid 1777, a priest in Lochaber, may have died in Arisaig, Halifax, Nova Scotia, on 15 April 1816. [IR.XVIII.154][SCP#218][RSC.I.206]

MACDONALD, ALEXANDER, born in Glen Urquhart, educated at Valladolid 1778, ordained at Valladolid by 1787, priest in Badenoch and Lochaber, then chaplain to the Glengarry Fencibles, emigrated to Canada in 1804, Bishop there, died in Dumfries, Scotland, on 14 January 1840. [IR.XVIII.160][RSC.I.207]

MACDONALD, ALEXANDER, born 1755, ordained in Rome 1782, a priest in Balloch, Edinburgh, and Crieff, died in Crieff on 31 July 1837.

MACDONALD NIC COUL, ALLAN, of Morar, Inverness-shire, 1703. [NAS.CH1.2.5.2]

MCDONALD, ALLAN, servant to the laird of Morar, Inverness-shire, 1703. [NAS.CH1.2.5.2]

MACDONALD, ALLAN, born around 1696, son of Alexander MacDonald of Stonybridge and Giles MacDonald, educated at the Scots College in Paris from 1715 to 1721, a schoolmaster in the Highlands, ordained in Scotland 1736, priest in Keppoch, a Jacobite in 1745, deported, returned to Scotland in 1768, died in Canongait on 17 May 1781. [IR.XVIII.140][SCP#216]

MACDONALD, ALLAN, from the Isles, ordained in Rome before 1767, schoolmaster at Buorblach and at Samalan, possibly a missionary on Eigg, died there 22 March 1788. [IR.XVIII.148][RSC.I.205]

MACDONALD, ALLAN, a student at the Scots College at Valladolid, 1785, DIED IN Edinburgh on 8 September 1793. [RSC.I.209]

MCDONALD, ANGUS, with four children, in Belgarva, South Uist, 1703. [NAS.CH1.2.5.2]

MCDONALD, ANGUS, in south west South Uist, 1703. [NAS.CH1.2.5.2]

MCDONALD, ANGUS, in Morar, Inverness-shire, brother of John McDonald in Suinsletter, 1703. [NAS.CH1.2.5.2]

MCDONALD, or COGGAN, ANGUS, his wife Janet McGrigor, their children John, Isabel, Margaret, Janet, and Anne, in Glengarden, Aberdeenshire, 1718. [NAS.CH1.2.47.271]

MACDONALD, ANGUS, born 1716, son of Angus MacDonald of Dallely, ordained in Rome during 1752, priest on Barra, died there in August 1762. [IR.XVIII.143]

MACDONALD, ANGUS, possibly from Retland, South Morar, a student at the Scots College in Valladolid, 1776, ordained there in 1782, priest in Kintail, died at Abertarf on 14 April 1784. [IR.XVIII.157][RSC.I.207]

MACDONALD, ANGUS, born 1757, ordained in 1791, schoolmaster at Samalaman, Lismore, and Barra, Rector of the Scots College in Paris, died there 3 January 1833. [IR.XVIII.163]

MACDONALD, ANGUS, born 1779, at Ratisbon Seminary, 1791-1792. [SIG#295][RSC.I.254]

MACDONALD, ANTONY, born 1770, priest in the Small Isles from 1782 until his death on Eigg 6 January 1843. [IR.XVIII.162]

MCDONALD, ARCHIBALD, a student at the Scots College at Valladolid, 1771, died 1813. [RSC.I.205]

MCDONALD, AUGUSTINE, a student at the Scots College at Valladolid, 1771, ordained 1780, a missionary in Strathdon, died at Scalan in 1782. [RSC.I.206]

MCDONALD, AUGUSTIN, in Pictou, Nova Scotia, 1802. [SCA.BL4.187.16]

MACDONALD, AUSTIN, ordained in Rome by 1769, priest in Knoydart and Moidart, emigrated to Nova Scotia in 1803, died at Tracadie in 1807. [IR.XVIII.149]

MACDONALD, AUSTIN, born 1770, priest in Strathglass, died in Aigas on 27 March 1812. [IR.XVIII.164]

MCDONALD, CHARLES, born 1742, son of Donald McDonald of Kinlochmoidart and Elizabeth Stewart, a student at Douai, 1751. [RSC.I.88]

MACDONALD, CHARLES, born 1774 in Moidart, a student at the Scots College at Valladolid, 1788, ordained there by 1798, priest in Arisaig, Knoydart, Morven, Glasgow, Badenoch, died in Borrodale on 8 October 1848. [IR.XVIII.167][RSC.I.210]

MCDONALD, DONALD, of Benbecula, 1703. [NAS.CH1.2.5.2]

MCDONALD, DONALD, a student at the Scots College at Valladolid, 1771. [SC.I.206]

MACDONALD, DONALD, son of MacDonald of Iren, ordained at Douai in 1782, schoolmaster at Samalaman from 1782 until his death on 22 January 1785. [IR.XVII.52; XVIII.157]

MACDONALD, DUGALD, born in Uist around 1720, ordained in Rome possibly in 1746, a priest in Uist, died there 1 October 1751. [IR.XVIII.142]

MACDONALD, EVAN, a student at the Scots College at Valladolid, 1788, later a missionary in Braemar. [RSC.I.210]

MACDONALD, FRANCIS, from Glengarry, ordained at Scalan in 1736, a priest in Moidart, Badenoch, and Eigg, abandoned Catholicism in 1743, settled in Skye, died around 1777. [IR.XVIII.137]

MCDONALD, HUGH, born in Morar, ordained at Scalan in 1725, priest in Morar, a Jacobite in 1745 – escaped to France but returned in 1749, banished in 1755 but returned to Scotland, based at Auchintoul, Banffshire, died at Aberchallader, Glengarry, Inverness-shire, 1774. [IR.XVIII.133]

MCDONALD, HUGH, 'a trafficking papist', banished, 1756. [NAS.HCR.I.89]

MCDONALD, JAMES, of Arde, with four children, in Sleat, Skye, 1703. [NAS.CH1.2.5.1]

MCDONALD, JAMES, born 1736, ordained in Rome during 1765, a Catholic priest from Moidart, emigrated on the brig <u>Alexander of Greenock</u> in June 1772, landed at Charlottetown, Prince Edward Island, 25 June 1772, died there in April 1785. [SCA.BL3.242/2; BL3.2.288/9-10][IR.XVII.50; XVIII.147]

MCDONALD, JAMES, in Guidal, 1790. [SCA.BL.4.32.10]

MACDONALD, JAMES HUGH, born in Guidal, Morar, educated at the Scots College in Paris 1764, ordained in Paris 1770, schoolmaster at Buorblach, the priest in Knoydart, Morar, and the Small Isles, emigrated to Prince Edward Island in 1791, died in Quebec during 1807. [IR.XVIII.150][SCP#218]

MACDONALD, JAMES ALLAN, ordained 1792, priest in Strathglass, Balloch, and Barra, died either in 1801 or 1803. [IR.XVIII.164]

MCDONALD, JAMES, a student at the Scots College at Douai, 1793. [IR.LVIII.223]

MCDONALD, JOHN, of Beusdill, South Uist, 1703. [NAS.CH1.2.5.2]

MCDONALD, JOHN, with two children in Dallborrou, South Uist, 1703. [NAS.CH1.2.5.2]

MCDONALD, JOHN, in Suinsletter, Morar, Inverness-shire, 1703. [NAS.CH1.2.5.2]

MACDONALD, JOHN, a schoolmaster from Lochaber, ordained in Rome around 1730, a priest in Lochaber, died there in 1761. [IR.XVIII.133]

MACDONALD, JOHN, born 1727 in Ardnamurchan, ordained in Rome during 1753, priest in Uist until 1761, died in Knoydart on 9 May 1779. [IR.XVIII.144]

MACDONALD, JOHN, born in Menteith, Perthshire, during 1752, a student at the Scots College at Valladolid, 1771, ordained there around 1776, priest in Moidart, Barra, and Arisaig, died at Rinaleoid, Arisaig, on 7 July 1834. [IR.XVII.51; XVIII.153][RSC.I.205]

MCDONALD, JOHN, a student at the Scots College at Valladolid, 1788, later in America. [RSC.I.210]

MCDONALD, LACHLAN, in Eigg, Inverness-shire, 1703. [NAS.CH1.2.5.2]

MCDONALD, MARJORY, in Fochabers, 1710. [NAS.CH1.2.29.3/210]

MCDONALD, MORE, in Forme, in Glenmuick, Tullich, and Glengarden, Aberdeenshire, 1718. [NAS.CH1.2.47/284]

MCDONALD, NORMAN, ordained in Rome in 1780, a priest in Uist, Arisaig, and Moidart, died 1837. [IR.XVIII.155]

MCDONALD, PETER, in Fochabers, Morayshire, 1705; in Abertarff and Glencairn, 1714. [NAS.CH1.2.5/2] [NLS.ms976.143]

MCDONALD, PETER, a weaver, with wife Catherine Smith, in Parish of Bellie, 1710. [NAS.CH1.2.29.3/211]

MCDONALD, RANALD, in Trotternish, Skye, brother of Coll McDonald, 1703. [NAS.CH1.2.5.2]

MCDONALD, RANALD, of Kinbeathy, Trotternish, Skye, 1703. [NAS.CH1.2.5.2]

MCDONALD, RANALD, of Cross, Morar, Inverness-shire, brother to Allan McDonald, 1703. [NAS.CH1.2.5.2]

MCDONALD, RANALD, in Inverosy, Morar, Inverness-shire, 1703. [NAS.CH1.2.5.2]

MCDONALD, RANALD, tenant of Aberarder on the forfeited estate of Cluny, was 'turned out as a papist' in 1726. [NAS.GD44.27.10]

MACDONALD, RANALD, son of Ranald MacDonald, 15th Chief of Clanranald, and Margaret McLeod, educated at the Scots College in Paris from 1739 to 1742, married (1) Mary Hamilton, (2) Flora Mackinnon. [SCP#217]

MCDONALD, RONALD, son of Archibald McDonald of Barisdale, guilty of enlisting in French Service, banished 13 August 1754. [NAS.HCR.I.87]

MCDONALD, RANALD, born 1754, a student at the Scots College in Valladolid, 1771, ordained at Valladolid in 1780, priest in Morar, died there on 25 December 1840. [IR.XVIII.155][RSC.I.206]

MCDONALD, RANALD, at Scothouse, Inverness-shire, 1782. [SCA.OL.6.1.1]

MACDONALD, RANALD, born 1756 in Edinburgh, ordained in Douai by 1782, priest in Glencairn, Glengarry, and Uist, Vicar Apostolic from 1820, died at Fort William on 20 September 1832. [IR.XVIII.157]

MACDONALD, RODERICK, born 1763 , from Garrfluich, South Uist, a student at the Scots College in Valladolid, 1780, ordained in Edinburgh 1791, priest in Badenoch, South Uist and Benbecula, died there 29 September 1828. [IR.XVIII.163]

MCDONALD, RORIE, a servant in Fochabers, Morayshire, 1705. [NAS.CH1.2.5/2]

MCDONALD, SOIRLE, with two children, in Gerrifliuch, South Uist, 1703. [NAS.CH1.2.5.2]

MCDONALD, ..., child of the late Alexander McDonald of Stonbridge, in South Uist, 1763. [NAS.CH1.2.5.2]

MCDONALD, ..., child of the late John McDonald of Kildaunen, in South Uist, 1703. [NAS.CH1.2.5.2]

MCDONALD, ..., a schoolmaster in Auchriachan, 1720. [NLS.ms68.fo.31-32]

MCDONALD, ..., of Kiltrie, 1714. [NLS.ms976.143]

MCDONELL, ALEXANDER, of Muckerah, Inverness-shire, 1703. [NAS.CH1.2.5.2]

MCDONELL, ALEXANDER, in Ardnafouram, Arisaig, Inverness-shire, 1703. [NAS.CH1.2.5.2]

MCDONELL, ALEXANDER, son of the late Donald McDonell of Scotus, brother of the laird of Glengarry, in Glenelg and Knoydart, 1703. [NAS.CH1.2.5.2]

MCDONELL, ALEXANDER, the younger of Borradaill, Arisaig, Inverness-shire, 1703. [NAS.CH1.2.5.2]

MACDONELL, ALEXANDER, of Glengarry, Inverness-shire, 1703. [NAS.CH1.2.5.2]

MACDONELL, ALEXANDER, of Kytrie, Glengarry, Inverness-shire, 1703. [NAS.CH1.2.5.2]

MACDONELL, ALEXANDER, in Achaloucharah, Glengarry, Inverness-shire, 1703. [NAS.CH1.2.5.2]

MACDONELL, ALEXANDER, in Munerogie, Glengarry, Inverness-shire, 1703. [NAS.CH1.2.5.2]

MACDONELL, ALEXANDER, in Clasnacarich, Glengarry, Morar, Inverness-shire, 1703. [NAS.CH1.2.5.2]

MACDONELL, ALEXANDER, at Ratisbon Seminary, 1764. [SIG#295][RSC.I.253]

MCDONELL, ALLAN, of Moidart, Inverness-shire, 1703. [NAS.CH1.2.5.2]

MCDONELL, ALLAN, in Skearie, Knoydart, Inverness-shire, 1703. [NAS.CH1.2.5.2]

MACDONELL, ALLAN, in Ardglash, Glengarry, Morar, Inverness-shire, 1703. [NAS.CH1.2.5.2]

MCDONELL, ALLAN, a student at the Scots College at Valladolid, 1778. [RSC.I.208]

MCDONELL, ALLAN, born 1754, farmer at Cask of Inverchannich, died 14 March 1826, husband of Eliza Chisholm, born 1754, died in April 1824. [Clachan Comair Monumental Inscription, Kerrow, Inverness-shire]

MACDONELL, ANGUS, of Scatah, Knoydart, Inverness-shire, 1703. [NAS.CH1.2.5.2]

MACDONELL, ANGUS, of Octerae, Glengarry, Inverness-shire, 1703. [NAS.CH1.2.5.2]

MACDONELL, ANGUS, son of Ranald MacDonald in Pitmean, Glengarry, Inverness-shire, 1703. [NAS.CH1.2.5.2]

MCDONELL, ANGUS, of Tullich, Trotternish, Skye, Inverness-shire, 1703. [NAS.CH1.2.5.2]

MCDONELL, ANGUS, son of Alexander McDonell of Muckerah, Inverness-shire, 1703. [NAS.CH1.2.5.2]

MCDONELL, ANGUS, brother of Ranald McDonell of Kinloch Moidart, Inverness-shire, 1703. [NAS.CH1.2.5.2]

MCDONELL, ANGUS, in Essan, Moidart, Inverness-shire, 1703. [NAS.CH1.2.5.2]

MCDONELL, ARCHIBALD, in Knoydart, Inverness-shire, 1703. [NAS.CH1.2.5.2]

MCDONELL, AUGUSTINE, a student at the Scots College at Valladolid, 1788. [RSC.I.210]

MCDONELL, CHARLES, at Ratisbon Seminary, 1764. [SIG#295][RSC.I.253]

MCDONELL, DONALD, son of the late Donald McDonell of Scotus, brother of the laird of Glengarry, in Glenelg and Knoydart, 1703. [NAS.CH1.2.5.2]

MACDONELL, DONALD, brother to the late Bellfinlay, in Arisaig, Inverness-shire, 1703. [NAS.CH1.2.5.2]

MACDONELL, DONALD, of Wester Aberchalder, Glengarry, Inverness-shire, 1703. [NAS.CH1.2.5.2]

MACDONELL, DONALD, of Lundie, Knoydart, Inverness-shire, 1703. [NAS.CH1.2.5.2]

MCDONNELL, FRANCIS, an Irish Franciscan priest from Armagh to the Hebrides in 1671. [IR.XXIII.53; XXIV.76]

MCDONELL, ISABEL, died at Kerrow in 1816, spouse to Colin Chisholm. [Clachan Comar MI. Kilmorack]

MCDONELL, JAMES, of Bellfinlay, Arisaig, Inverness-shire, 1703. [NAS.CH1.2.5.2]

MACDONELL, JAMES, of Culleachie the younger, Glengarry, Inverness-shire, 1703. [NAS.CH1.2.5.2]

MCDONELL, JOHN, son of Rorie McDonell of Glenaldaill, Moidart, Inverness-shire, 1703. [NAS.CH1.2.5.2]

MCDONELL, JOHN, in Essan, Moidart, Inverness-shire, 1703. [NAS.CH1.2.5.2]

MACDONELL, JOHN, of Shian, Glengarry, Inverness-shire, 1703. [NAS.CH1.2.5.2]

MACDONELL, JOHN, of Ardnabie, Glengarry, Inverness-shire, 1703. [NAS.CH1.2.5.2]

MACDONELL, JOHN, son of Ronald McDonell of Glengarry, Knoydart, Inverness-shire, 1703. [NAS.CH1.2.5.2]

MCDONELL, JOHN, of Leek, Glengarry, Inverness-shire, 1703. [NAS.CH1.2.5.2]

MACDONELL, JOHN, the younger, of Wester Aberchalder, Glengarry, Inverness-shire, 1703. [NAS.CH1.2.5.2]

MCDONELL, JOHN, at Ratisbon Seminary 1719. [SIG#294]

MCDONELL, JOHN, at Ratisbon Seminary 1735. [RSC.I.251]

MCDONELL, JOHN, at Ratisbon Seminary 1756. [SIG#294]

MCDONELL, MARGARET, daughter of the late Donald McDonell of Scotus, brother of the laird of Glengarry, in Glenelg and Knoydart, 1703. [NAS.CH1.2.5.2]

MCDONELL, RANALD, brother of Allan McDonell, in Moidart, Inverness-shire, 1703. [NAS.CH1.2.5.2]

MACDONELL, RANALD, of Culleachie, Glengarry, Inverness-shire, 1703. [NAS.CH1.2.5.2]

MACDONELL, RANALD, in Pitmean, Glengarry, Inverness-shire, 1703. [NAS.CH1.2.5.2]

MACDONELL, RANALD, of Glengarry, Knoydart, Inverness-shire, 1703. [NAS.CH1.2.5.2]

MCDONELL, RANALD, of Kinloch Moidart, Inverness-shire, 1703. [NAS.CH1.2.5.2]

MACDONELL, or MCALISTER, RONALD, in Glengarry, Inverness-shire, 1703. [NAS.CH1.2.5.2]

MACDONELL, RANALD, of Barastill, Knoydart, Inverness-shire, 1703. [NAS.CH1.2.5.2]

MACDONELL, RODERICK, son of John MacDonell of Leek, ordained in Douai before 1775, priest in Glengarry from 1775 until 1785, emigrated to Quebec and the St Regis Iroquois mission. [IR.XVIII.152]

MCDONELL, RONALD, in Essan, Moidart, Inverness-shire, 1703. [NAS.CH1.2.5.2]

MCDONELL, RORIE, in Moidart, Inverness-shire, 1703. [NAS.CH1.2.5.2]

MCDONELL, RORIE, of Glenaldaill, Moidart, Inverness-shire, 1703. [NAS.CH1.2.5.2]

MCDONELL, WILLIAM, at Ratisbon Seminary 1726. [SIG#294]

MACDONNELL, ALASTAIR RUADH, born 1725, son of John MacDonnell, 12th Chief of Glengarry, and Margaret McKenzie, educated at the Scots College in Paris 1740, died unmarried in 1761. [SCP#217]

MCDONNELL, CATHERINE, sister of Francis MacDonald priest of Moidart and Ardnamurchan, 1743. [NAS.CH1.2.84.fos.228-244]

MCDOUGAL, JAMES, with his wife Anne Coutts, three daughters and three sons, in Glenmuick, Tullich, and Glengarden, 1718. [NAS.CH1.2.47/284]

MCDOUGAL, JOHN, a student at the Scots College at Valladolid, 1780, later on St Vincent. [RSC.I.208]

MCDOWAL, BARBARA, in Glasgow 1703, and in Kilsyth, 1704. [NAS.CH1.2.5.1/3/184]

MCDUGAL, ALEXANDER, his wife Isobel Kerr, 2 sons and 3 daughters, in Tomnafiagh, Glengarden, Aberdeenshire, 1718. [NAS.CH1.2.47.271]

MACEACHAN, ANGUS BERNARD, a student at the Scots College at Valladolid, 1777, ordained there by 1787, priest in the Small Isles, emigrated to Prince Edward Island in 1790, Bishop of Charlottetown, died there 22 April 1835. [IR.XVIII.160][RSC.I.207]

MCEACHAN, DONALD, with two children, in South Uist, 1703. [NAS.CH1.2.5.2]

MCEACHAN, HECTOR, of Peinninreine, South Uist, 1703. [NAS.CH1.2.5.2]

MCEACHEN, JOHN, of Houbegg, South Uist, and two children, 1703. [NAS.CH1.2.5.2]

MACEACHAN, RANALD, from the Isles, born 1756, ordained in Rome by 1782, priest on Uist, died in South Uist or Barra in 1803. [IR.XVIII.157]

MCEACHRAN, ANGUS, in Savage Harbour, Canada, 1791. [SCA.BL4.33.11]

MCEAN VIC ANGUS, WILLIAM, and family, in Guisachan, Kiltarlity, Inverness-shire, 1710. [NAS.CH1.2.29.3]

MCEAN VIC COY, JOHN, and family, in Guisachan, Kiltarlity, Inverness-shire, 1710. [NAS.CH1.2.29.3]

MCEAN VIC KERIE, DONALD, and family, in Kirkton of Comar, Kiltarlity, Inverness-shire, 1710. [NAS.CH1.2.29.3]

MCEAN, HUTCHEON, a miller in Guisachen, an apostate in Kiltarlity, 1679. [IR.XXIV.82]

MCEUN VIC QUEEN, DONALD, and his family, in Guisachan, Kiltarlity, Inverness-shire, 1710. [NAS.CH1.2.29.3]

MCEUN, JOHN, Strathaven, Banffshire, 1708. [NAS.CH1.2.30/1/28]

MCFADZEAN, JANET, and daughters Marion and Isobel Sturgeon, in Troquair, Orr, Dumfries-shire, 1705. [NAS.CH1.2.5/156]

MCFIE, NEIL, born in South Uist, ordained in Rome 1726, a priest in Uist, Arasaig, and by 1738 in Barra, died in 1774. [IR.XVIII.134]

MCFINLAY, CHRISTOPHER, with his family of three or four, in Kirkton of Comar, Kiltarlity, Inverness-shire, 1710. [NAS.CH1.2.29.3]

MCGAREUCK, CHARLES, a servant to the Earl of Nithsdale, Terregles, Dumfries-shire, 1703. [NAS.CH1.2.5.1]

MCGIBBON, MARGARET, in Balloch, Auchterarder, Perthshire, 1703. [NAS.CH1.2.5.2]

MCGIE, BARBARA, a servant in Buittle, Kirkcudbrightshire, 1705. [NAS.CH1.2.5.2]

MCGIE, JOHN, a servant in Buittle, Kirkcudbrightshire, 1705. [NAS.CH1.2.5.2]

MCGIE, JANET, daughter of the late James McGie a cottar in Buittle, Kirkcudbrightshire, 1705. [NAS.CH1.2.5.2]

MCGILL, MARGARET, in Cargill, Perthshire, 1704. [NAS.CH1.2.5.3.203]

MCGILL, ROBERT, in Troquair, Orr, Dumfries-shire, 1705. [NAS.CH1.2.5/156]

MCGILL, WILLIAM, rector of the Scots College in Madrid, 1727-1734. [RSC.I.203]

MCGILLICHALLUM, NIEL, in Duchamis, Arisaig, Inverness-shire, 1703. [NAS.CH1.2.5.2]

MCGILLIES, DONALD, in Romasaik, Glengarry, Morar, Inverness-shire, 1703. [NAS.CH1.2.5.2]

MCGILLIES, JOHN, in Ardnamurchan, Inverness-shire, 1703. [NAS.CH1.2.5.2]

MCGILLIES or MCCOIL, NIEL, in Morar, Inverness-shire, 1703. [NAS.CH1.2.5.2]

MCGILLIES, WILLIAM, in Kinloch Morar, Inverness-shire, 1703. [NAS.CH1.2.5.2]

MCGILLIS, ANGUS, from the Hebrides, ordained in Rome during 1739, a priest in Glengarry, a Jacobite at Culloden in 1745, later in Barra, Glengarry and Lochaber, died 9 August 1776. [IR.XVIII.138]

MCGILLIS, ANGUS, born 1745, ordained in Rome by 1772, schoolmaster at Buorblach and Lochaber, priest in Lochaber from 1776 until his death in 1812. [IR.XVIII.151]

MCGILLISPICK, THOMAS, and his family, in Kiltarlity, Inverness-shire, 1710. [NAS.CH1.2.29.3]

MCGILLIVIE, JOHN, miller at Castleton, Braemar, Aberdeenshire, 1713. [NAS.GD124.15.1098.1]

MCGILLIVRAY, ANGUS, a student at the Scots College at Valladolid, 1777, died 21 June 1778. [SC.I.207]

MCGILLIVRAY or FARQUHARSON, JAMES, born 28 December 1749, son of Farquhar McGillivray and Helen Keith, a student at Douai 1763. [RSC.I.92]

MACGREGOR, CALUM, at Ratisbon Seminary 1719. [SIG#294][RSC.I.251]

MCGREGOR, JOHN, and his spouse Christian Grant in Strathaven, Banffshire, 1708. [NAS.CH1.2.30/1/28]

MCGRIGOR, JOHN, in Mullach, with his wife Beatrix McGrigor, and his son Euan and a daughter, in Glenmuick, Tullich, and Glengarden, Aberdeenshire, 1718. [NAS.CH1.2.47/284]

MCGREGOR, MARGARET, in the Muir of Glengarden, Aberdeenshire, 1718. [NAS.CH1.2.47.271]

MCGREGOR, JOHN, and his wife Beatrix Grant, in Keppoch, Strathaven, Banffshire, 1708. [NAS.CH1.2.30/1/28]

MCGRIGOR, ANNE, housekeeper to Father Ramsay, in Ardach, in Glenmuick, Tullich, and Glengarden, Aberdeenshire, 1718. [NAS.CH1.2.47/284]

MCGRIGOR, COLLIN or CALUM, in Dalfaed, Glengardyne, Kincardineshire, 1710. [NAS.CH1.2.29.3]

MCGRIGOR, ELSPET, a servant in Foran, Glengarden, Aberdeenshire, 1718. [NAS.CH1.2.47.271]

MCGRIGOR, ELSPET, a servant in Riahloin, 1718. [NAS.CH1.2.7.271]

MCGRIGOR, GEORGE, with his wife Janet Grassich, and two children, in Dalfad, in Glenmuick, Tullich, and Glengarden, Aberdeenshire, 1718. [NAS.CH1.2.47/284]

MCGRIGOR, GRIGOR, a smith, 'a late apostate, his wife Mary Duvard, and son John, in Glengarden, Aberdeenshire, 1718. [NAS.CH1.2.47.271]

MCGRIGOR, or BAIN, GRIGOR, with his wife Janet, also his son John with his wife Isabel and two children, in Glenmuick, Tullich, and Glengarden, Aberdeenshire, 1718. [NAS.CH1.2.47/284]

MCGRIGOR, JANET, in Rianetten, Tullich, Aberdeenshire, 1718. [NAS.CH1.2.7.271]

MCGRIGOR, JOHN, and his wife, in Micras, Tullich, Aberdeenshire, 1718. [NAS.CH1.2.7.271]

MCGRIGOR, JOHN, with his wife Anne Michy and one child, in Glenmuick, Tullich, and Glengarden, Aberdeenshire, 1718. [NAS.CH1.2.47/284]

MCGRIGOR, NEIL, in Lairy, in Glenmuick, Tullich, and Glengarden, Aberdeenshire, 1718. [NAS.CH1.2.47/284]

MCGRIOR, ALEXANDER, his wife Margaret, and 3 children, in Morvine, 1718. [NAS.CH1.2.7.271]

MCHALLIE, JAMES, a gardener in Banff, Banffshire, 1794. [NAS.SC2.72.4]

MACHALNE, ALEXANDER, in Burnfield,Kinnore parish, 1710. [NAS.CH1.2.29.3/210]

MACHALNE, JOHN, the younger, in Kinnore parish, 1710. [NAS.CH1.2.29.3/210]

MCHARDIE, JOHN, a tailor in Tomnafiagh, with his mother Janet Fleming, in Glengarden, Aberdeenshire, 1718. [NAS.CH1.2.47.271]

MCHATTIE, JOHN, a student at the Scots College in Valladolid, 1771, died April 1774. [RSC.I.205]

MCHUTCHEON, ALEXANDER, a smith in Guisachan, an apostate in Kiltarlity, 1679. [IR.XXIV.82]

MCHUTCHEON, DUNCAN, an apostate in Comar, Kiltarlity, 1679. [IR.XXIV.82]

MCHUTCHEON MOIR, THOMAS, in Kilmorack, 1673. [IR.XXIV.80]

MCHUTCHEON, WILLIAM, in Comar, an apostate in Kiltarlity, 1679. [IR.XXIV.82]

MCILDUFF, JOHN, and wife Margaret, in Orr, Dumfries-shire, 1705.[NAS.CH1.2.5/156]

MCILIVRIE, JOHN, his wife Janet Michie, 1 son and 3 daughters in Foran, Glengarden, Aberdeenshire, 1718. [NAS.CH1.2.47.271]

MCILIVRIE, MARY, wife to John McHardie, with his mother-in-law Elspet Tause, in Ardach, in Glenmuick, Tullich, and Glengarden, Aberdeenshire, 1718. [NAS.CH1.2.47/284]

MACINTOSH, DONALD, born 1732, at Ratisbon Seminary in 1739. [SIG#294][RSC.I.252]

MCINTOSH, JOHN, born in Corymulzie on 20 August 1747, died at Lary on 27 May 1797, husband of Mary Farquharson, born 1767, died 16 February 1847. [Braemar MI]

MCINTOSH, LACHLAN, born 1752, a student at the Scots College in Valladolid, 1771, ordained in Segovia in 1782, priest in Glencairn, died there 9 March 1846. [IR.XVIII.157][RSC.I.205]

MCINTYRE, JOHN, born 1783 on South Uist, died 18 November 1857 on Cape Breton Island, his wife Catherine, born 1785 on South Uist, died 13 July 1857 on Cape Breton Island. [St Andrew's RC Cemetery, Boisdale, Cape Breton]

MCISAAC, JAMES, and his wife Janet Grant, in Strathaven, Banffshire, 1708. [NAS.CH1.2.30/1/28]

MCIVER, ARCHIBALD, born 1780, at Ratisbon Seminary 1791-1792. [SIG#295][RSC.I.254]

MCIVER, CHARLES, born 1743, son of William McIver and Lucy Van Der Sippen, a student at Douai, 1752. [RSC.I.89]

MCIVER, EVANDER, a merchant burgess, an apostate and a 'papist' and his wife, in Tron Kirk parish, later in West Kirk parish, Edinburgh, 1704. [NAS.CH1.2.5.2/149]

MCIVER, EVANDER, a merchant burgess in Mitchell's Close, with his wife and child, West Kirk parish, Edinburgh, 1704. [NAS.CH1.2.5.154]

MCIVER, ISOBEL, wife to Achannacie, Parish of Bellie, 1710. [NAS.CH1.2.29.3/211]

MCIVER, JOHN, born 29 July 1745, a student at Douai, 1757. [RSC.I.90]

MCIVOR, DONALD, in Kilmorack, Inverness-shire, 1673. [IR.XXIV.80]

MCIVOR, DONALD, in Erchless, an apostate in Kiltarlity, Inverness-shire, 1679. [IR.XXIV.82]

MCIVOR, RODERICK, in Maald, an apostate in Kiltarlity, Inverness –shire, 1679. [IR.XXIV.82]

MACKAVIE, ISOBEL, in Fochabers, Morayshire, 1705. [NAS.CH1.2.5/2]

MCKENZIE, ALEXANDER, son of the Earl of Seaforth, a student at the Scots College at Douai, 1685. [RSC.I.57]

MCKENZIE, COLIN, of Barnhill, and his son Alexander, in Pluscarden, Morayshire, 1705. [NAS.CH1.2.5/2]

MCKENZIE, DONALD, son of Donald McKenzie and Anna MacKenzie, a student at Douai 1758. [ESC.I.91]

MCKENZIE, GEORGE, of Kildun, tacksman of Aignish, Lewis, 1680s, father of Colin. [IR.XXIV.100]

MCKENZIE, JEAN, in Achintoul, Tullich, Aberdeenshire, 1718. [NAS.CH1.2.7.271]

MACKENZIE, KENNETH, born 1714, son of Hector and Joanna McKenzie, a student at the Scots College in Madrid, 1722, formerly a Jesuit, a priest in Strathglass, Inverness-shire, from 1756 to 1775, died in Aberdeen during 1775. [IR.XVIII.152][RSC.I.200]

MCKERCHAR, JOHN, in Gibstoun, Kinnoir parish, 1710. [NAS.CH1.2.29.3/210]

MACKIE, BONIFACE, born 1658, to Wurzburg in 1677, ordained in 1682, died in Edinburgh during 1712. [SF#281]

MCKIE, JAMES, in Muir of Tullich, Aberdeenshire, 1714. [NLS.ms976.143]

MCKNISH, AGNES, a servant in Kelton, Kirkcudbrightshire, 1705. [NAS.CH1.2.5.2]

MACLACHLAN, ANGUS or AENEAS, from the diocese of Argyll, educated at the Scots College in Paris from 1704 to 1712, ordained in Paris during 1712, a priest in Glengarry, Inverness-shire, later in Morar and at Scotus, died in March 1760. [IR.XVIII.133; XXIV.93] [NLS.ms976.143][SCP#213]

MCLACHLAN, DUGALL, and family, in Kirkton of Comar, Kiltarlity, Inverness-shire, 1710. [NAS.CH1.2.29.3]

MCLAGAN, JANET, and her daughters Isabel Sturgeon and Marion Sturgeon, in Mabie, Traquair, Dumfries-shire, 1703. [NAS.CH1.2.5.1]

MCLAUCHLAN, JOHN, a priest in Strathglass or Glenmoriston, Inverness-shire, 1720. [NLS.ms68.31-32]

MCLEAN, ALLAN, junior, a stocking weaver in Banff, 1794. [NAS.SC2.72.4]

MCLEAN, ANNA, born 1768, daughter of McLean of Borreray, married Alexander Arnott a merchant in Edinburgh pre-1788, died in Edinburgh on 11 February 1860. [IR.XVIII.196]

MCLEAN, DONALD, and his wife Anna Riach, Strathaven, Banffshire, 1708. [NAS.CH1.2.30/1/28]

MCLEAN, JOHN,a stocking weaver in Banff, 1794. [NAS.SC2.72.4]

MCLEAN, THOMAS, tenant in Upper Dallachie, wit his wife Marjory Nicol, Parish of Bellie, 1710. [NAS.CH1.2.29.3/211]

MCLENNAN, CALUM, from Stornaway, at Ratisbon Monastery in 1689, and at Wurzburg from 1694. [SF#272]

MCLENNAN, MURDOCH, and his family of three, in Kirkton of Comar, Kiltarlity, Inverness-shire, 1710. [NAS.CH1.2.29.3]

MCLEOD, MURDO, with two children, in South Uist, 1703. [NAS.CH1.2.5.2]

MCLEOD, NORMAN, born 1717, son of Norman McLeod and Catherine MacIver, educated at Douai, a Jesuit in Tournai, priest in Strathglass, Inverness-shire, from 1753 until 1777, died in Edinburgh in 1777. [IR.XVIII.152]

MACLEOD, or MACHARDY, WILLIAM, a student at the Scots College at Valladolid, 1788, ordained at Valladolid by 1798, priest in Braemar, Aberdeenshire, until his death on 3 June 1809. [IR.XVIII.167][Braemar MI][RSC.I.1788]

MCMILLAN, JANET, in Terregles and Kirkgunzeon, Dumfries-shire, 1705. [NAS.CH1.2.5.2]

MCMORRIE, AGNES, in Barnbarrach, Colvend, Dumfries-shire, 1704. [NAS.CH1.2.5.2]

MCNAB, EDWARD, born 1741, son of Donald McNab and Susan ...., a student at Douai, 1752. [RSC.I.89]

MCNABB, JAMES, and family, in Erchles, Kiltarlity, Inverness-shire, 1710. [NAS.CH1.2.29.3]

MCNAB, JOHN, born 19 May 1744, a student at Douai 1757. [RSC.I.90]

MCNEIL, ..., of Barra, with five children, 1703. [NAS.CH1.2.5.2]

MCNEIL, ARCHIBALD, with two children, in Valslin, Barra, 1703. [NAS.CH1.2.5.2]

MCNEIL, DONALD, with two daughters of the late Hector McNeil of Vattersay, in Barra, 1703. [NAS.CH1.2.5.2]

MCNEIL, DONALD, with two children, in Tangasdale, Barra, 1703. [NAS.CH1.2.5.2]

MCNEIL, DONALD, with two children, in Grim, Barra, 1703. [NAS.CH1.2.5.2]

MCNEIL, JOHN, brother of the laird of Barra, with three children, 1703. [NAS.CH1.2.5.2]

MCNEIL, MURDO, with two children, in Grim, Barra, 1703. [NAS.CH1.2.5.2]

MCNEIL, MURDO, with four children, in Vattersay, Barra, 1703. [NAS.CH1.2.5.2]

MCNEIL, MURDO, brother of the laird of Barra, with children, in Barra, 1703. [NAS.CH1.2.5.2]

MCNEIL, NEIL, and family, in Kirkton of Comar, Kiltarlity, Inverness-shire, 1710. [NAS.CH1.2.29.3]

MCNEIL, RANALD, a student at the Scots College at Valladolid, 1780, died in the East Indies. [RSC.I.206]

MCNEIL, RODERICK, born on Barra 1793, died on Cape Breton Island, 6 November 1856, his wife Jane, born on Barra 1796, died on Cape Breton Island, 12 November 1867. [St Andrew's RC Cemetery, Boisdale, C,B.]

MCNIVEN, DUNCAN, in the Mill of Drummond, Auchterarder, Perthshire, 1703. [NAS.CH1.2.5.2]

MCNIVEN, WILLIAM, tenant of Lord Drummond in Dalclahick, Comrie, Perthshire, and his children, 1703. [NAS.CH1.2.5.2]

MCNOE, JOHN, in Kirkconnel, Dumfries-shire, 1703. [NAS.CH1.2.5.1]

MCPHERSON, ANNE, a servant in the Parish of Bellie, 1710. [NAS.CH1.2.29.3/211]

MCPHERSON, ELIZABETH, a tenant woman in Cottonhill, Parish of Bellie, 1710. [NAS.CH1.2.29.3/211]

MCPHERSON, JOHN, with his wife Janet Coutts and four children, in Ardach, in Glenmuick, Tullich, and Glengarden, Aberdeenshire, 1718. [NAS.CH1.2.47/284]

MCPHERSON, LAUCHLAN, was sent abroad for education in 1719. [NLS.ms68.31-32]

MACPHERSON, MARGARET, a servant of Boynd, parish of Bellie, 1710. [NAS.CH1.2.29.3]

MACPHERSON, PAUL, born 1756, a student at the Scots College at Valladolid, 1777, died 24 November 1846. [RSC.I.207]

MACPHERSON, ROBERT, born 1780, educated at Ratisbon Seminary 1791-1792. [SIG#295][RSC.I.254]

MCPHERSON, THOMAS, and his wife Mary Haggon, at the Raws of Huntly, Dunbennan parish, 1710. [NAS.CH1.2.29.3/210]

MCPHERSON, WILLIAM, in Tullich, Glengarden, Aberdeenshire, 1718. [NAS.CH1.2.47.271]

MCPHIE, MALCOLM, a priest in the Outer Hebrides, 1720. [NLS.ms68.31-32]

MCRA, CHRISTOPHER, born 1764, a student at the Scots College at Valladolid, 1780, later in Kintail, died 27 September 1842. [RSC.I.209]

MCRAE, ALEXANDER, born 24 February 1672 in Kilmorack, Inverness-shire, son of Reverend John McRae an Episcopalian minister, educated at Douai, Tournai and Prague, returned to Scotland in 1703, a Jesuit priest in the Presbytery of Dingwall, 1707, died at Douai. [NAS.CH1.2/30/1/4][NLS.ms68.31][IR.XXIV.87]

MCRAE, PHILIP, born 1777, ordained as a priest in 1806, missionary at Fasnakyle, died 16 October 1842. [St Mary Eskadale MI]

MCRABBIE, JOHN, an officer to Lord Drummond, with his children in Auchterarder, Perthshire, 1703. [NAS.CH1.2.5.2]

MCRABBIE, WILLIAM, brother of the above, and his children, in Auchterarder, Perthshire, 1703. [NAS.CH1.2.5.2]

MACRAE, CHRISTOPHER, born 1764, ordained at Valladolid by 1787, priest in Kintail, Wester Ross, until his death on 27 September 1842. [IR.XVIII.160]

MCRORIE, JOHN, and his wife Margaret Munro, apostates in Comar, Kiltarlity, Inverness-shire, 1679. [IR.XXIV.82]

MCWILLIAM, FARQUHAR, and his wife Beatrix, apostates in Comar, Kiltarlity, Inverness-shire, 1679. [IR.XXIV.82]

MCWILLIE, JANET, in the parish of Bellie, 1710. [NAS.CH1.2.29.3/211]

MAIR, WILLIAM, tenant in Bray's, with his wife Marjory Achamachie, parish of Bellie, 1710. [NAS.CH1.2.29.3]

MAITLAND, ALEXANDER, brother to the Earl of Lauderdale, dwelling in Ardounie, 'a papist' in Angus, 1705. [NAS.CH1.2.5.2.171]

MAITLAND, Captain JAMES, and his spouse Margaret Elphinstone, also their children Charles, Ludovick, Elizabeth, and Janet, in Edinburgh, apostates and 'papists' in Nether Bow, College Kirk parish, Edinburgh, 1703/1704/ 1705. Their nearest Protestant relations are Maitland of Pitrothie and Elphinstone of Quarrell. [NAS.CH1.2.5.2.149/151/171]

MAITLAND, ROBERT, a Jesuit and a 'trafficking priest', 4 March 1751. [NAS.HCR.I.82]

MALCOLM, JAMES, withhis wife Jean Mearns, and Elspet Malcolm, at the Raws of Huntly, Dunbennan parish, 1710. [NAS.CH1.2.29.3/210]

MALCOLM, WILLIAM, late servitor to the Earl of Moray, and his spouse Anne Malcolm, 'papists' in Canongait, Edinburgh, 1703/1704/1705. [NAS.CH1.2.5.2.149/151/170]

MALCOLM, WILLIAM, from the Highlands, a student at the Scots College at Douai, 1793. [IR.LVIII.223][SCA.BL4.71.10]

MARK, PETER, in Greenfold, Kinnoir parish, 1710. [NAS.CH1.2.29.3/210]

MARTIN, ELIZABETH, relict of Charles McCormack, and their daughter Mary McCormack, in Canongait, Edinburgh,1703. [NAS.CH1.2.5.2/151]

MASSIE, JAMES, a merchant in Aberdeen, son of the late George Massie and his wife Margaret Oliphant, was baptised as a Protestant when young, and as a Catholic by Father Robert Francis in Aberdeen on 18 December 1697. [SNQ.VIII.182]

MASSON, JAMES, at Ratisbon Seminary 1713. [SIG#294][RSC.I.250]

MATHESON, ELSPET, in Ruthven, Strathbogie,1710. [NAS.CH1.2.29.3/209]

MATHESON, GEORGE, a subtenant in Cumry, and his wife Margaret Sharp, in Ruthven, Strathbogie,1710. [NAS.CH1.2.29.3/209]

MATHESON, GEORGE, born 1756, a student at the Scots College in Valladolid, 1771, died at the mission of Auchenarlie on 14 January 1828. [RSC.I.205]

MATHEWSON, JAMES, a tenant in Upper Achinroth, with his wife Agnes Leith, in the parish of Bellie, 1710. [NAS.CH1.2.29.3/211]

MAXWELL, AGNES, in Greencaple, Caerlaverock, Dumfries-shire, 1705. [NAS.CH1.2.5.1]

MAXWELL, AGNES, spouse to Alexander Brown of Kempletoun(?), an their sons .... (in France) and ...... (in Aberdeen), in Twynholm, Kirkcudbrightshire, 1705. [NAS.CH1.2.5.2]

MAXWELL, AGNES, sister to James Maxwell of Kirkconnel, New Abbey, Dumfries-shire, 1703. [NAS.CH1.2.5.1]

MAXWELL, BARBARA, of Munches, relict of George Maxwell of Munches, in Buittle, Kirkcudbrightshire, 1705. [NAS.CH1.2.5.2]

MAXWELL, BERNARD, born 1641, Abbot of Wurzburg from 1679 to his death in 1685. [SF#272-280]

MAXWELL, BETTY, sister to James Maxwell of Kirkconnel, New Abbey, Dumfries-shire, 1703. [NAS.CH1.2.5.1]

MAXWELL, CATHERINE, a servant in Traquair, Peebles-shire, 1705. [NAS.CH1.2.5.3/176]

MAXWELL, CHARLES, a gentleman in Terregles, Dumfries-shire, 1705. [NAS.CH1.2.5.2]

MAXWELL, CHARLES, born 1748, a student at Douai, 1761. [RSC.I.92]

MAXWELL, CHARLES, in Black Friars Wynd, Edinburgh, 1802. [SCA.BL.4.187.16]

MAXWELL, CHRISTIAN, and her daughter Mary Drummond, in Tron Kirk parish, Edinburgh, 1703. [NAS.CH1.2.5.2/151]

MAXWELL, DAVID, a cottar in Orchardton, with his daughter Agnes, in Buittle, Kirkcudbrightshire, 1705. [NAS.CH1.2.5.2]

MAXWELL, ELIZABETH, servant to Sir George Seton at Garleton, East Lothian, and her daughters Clara aged 16 and Elizabeth Maxwell aged 14, both servants there, 1703. [NAS.CH1.2.5.1]

MAXWELL, ELIZABETH, spouse to Dr Alexander, and her daughter Mary Drummond, ' papists' in Canongait parish, Edinburgh, 1704/1705. [NAS.CH1.2.5.2.140/170]

MAXWELL, ELIZABETH, relict of Robert Maxwell of Kirkhouse, in Kirkbean, Orr, Dumfries-shire, 1705. [NAS.CH1.2.5/156]

MAXWELL, ELIZABETH, a cottar in Barlochan, in Buittle, Kirkcudbrightshire, 1705. [NAS.CH1.2.5.2]

MAXWELL, FRANCIS, son to the late John Maxwell of Carse, Dunscore, Dumfries, 1705. [NAS.CH1.2.5.1]

MAXWELL, FRANCIS, of Brock (?), and his spouse Barbara Maxwell, with daughters Margaret and Mary Maxwell, in Buittle, Kirkcudbrightshire, 1705. [NAS.CH1.2.5.2]

MAXWELL, GEORGE, of Carruchen, his wife Margaret Stewart, children Agnes, Henry, and Robert, also his mother Agnes Lindsay, in Troquair, Orr, Dumfries-shire, 1703/1705. [NAS.CH1.2.1.5/156]

MAXWELL, GEORGE, of Munches, with his spouse Katherine Maxwell, and children – William aged 16 (in France), George aged 15 (in France), James aged 10, and Mary aged 13, in Buittle, Kirkcudbrightshire, 1705. [NAS.CH1.2.5.2]

MAXWELL, HEW, in Knockins, his spouse Elizabeth Drummond, daughter Agnes, son David, in Terregles and Kirkgunzeon, Dumfries-shire, 1705. [NAS.CH1.2.5.2]

MAXWELL, JAMES, son of James Maxwell of Kirkconnell, a student at the Scots College at Douai, 1691. [RSC.I.61]

MAXWELL, JAMES, the younger of Barncluch, Lochmaben, Dumfries-shire, 1703. [NAS.CH1.2.5.1]

MAXWELL, JAMES, servant to John Ridge, New Abbey, Dumfries-shire, 1703. [NAS.CH1.2.5.1]

MAXWELL, JAMES, son of Robert Maxwell of Gelston, and his daughters Anna and Mary , in Buittle, Kirkcudbrightshire, 1705. [NAS.CH1.2.5.2]

MAXWELL, JAMES, of Munches, a Jacobite in 1745, fled to St Germains in 1746, returned to Scotland in 1755. [NAS.GD46.6.100]

MAXWELL, JAMES, born 1759, son of James Maxwell baron of Kirkconnell, a student at Douai, 1770. [RSC.I.94]

MAXWELL, JANET, spouse to John Crichton, in Troquair, Orr, Dumfries-shire, 1705. [NAS.CH1.2.5/156]

MAXWELL, JANET, spouse to John Gunzion a tenant farmer in Townhead of Kirkconnel, Dumfries-shire, 1703. [NAS.CH1.2.5.1]

MAXWELL, JANET, a tenant or cottar in Cargan, Traquair, Dumfries-shire, 1703. [NAS.CH1.2.5.1]

MAXWELL, JEAN, in Drimly of Kirkconnel, New Abbey, Dumfries-shire, 1703. [NAS.CH1.2.5.1]

MAXWELL, JOHN, of Barncleugh, liberated, 1690. [RPCS.XV.435]

MAXWELL, JOHN, born 22 August 1682, son of John Maxwell of Barncleugh, a student at the Scots College at Douai, 1698. [RSC.I.64]

MAXWELL, Major JOHN, in Terregles, Dumfries-shire, 1703. [NAS.CH1.2.5.1]

MAXWELL, JOHN, of Barnsheugh, his wife Margaret Young, and his daughter Mary in Dumfries, 1705. [NAS.CH1.2.5.1]

MAXWELL, JOHN, of Brackenford (?),in Buittle, Kirkcudbrightshire, 1705. [NAS.CH1.2.5.2]

MAXWELL, JOHN, son of the late John Maxwell of Carse, Dunscore, Dumfries-shire, 1705. [NAS.CH1.2.5.1]

MAXWELL, MARION, sister to the late laird of Kirkconnel, New Abbey, Dumfries-shire, 1703. [NAS.CH1.2.5.1]

MAXWELL, MARION, in Barnbarrach, Colvend, Dumfries-shire, 1704. [NAS.CH1.2.5.2]

MAXWELL, NICHOLAS, of Little Bar, New Abbey, Dumfries-shire, 1703. [NAS.CH1.2.5.1]

MAXWELL, ROBERT, of Kirkhouse, in Kirkbean, Dumfries-shire, 1704. [NAS.CH1.5.2]

MAXWELL, ROBERT, of Millentoun, in Buittle, Kirkcudbrightshire, 1705. [NAS.CH1.2.5.2]

MAXWELL, ROBERT, of Gelston, with his children George aged 22, Mungo aged 4, Elizabeth aged 2, in Kelton, Kirkcudbrightshire, 1705. [NAS.CH1.2.5.2]

MAXWELL, ROBERT, son of ..... Maxwell, a student at Douai, 1747. [RSC.I.86]

MAXWELL, STEPHEN, a priest and master of the 'popish college' in Holyroodhouse, a prisoner in Lanark and in Edinburgh tolbooths, 1690. [RPCS.XV.496]

MAXWELL, THOMAS, a tenant farmer in Aird of Kirkconnel, and his wife Elizabeth Irvine, daughters Agnes aged 14, Mary aged 10, Lucie aged 6, and

Elizabeth aged 4, sons James aged 8, and William aged 12, in New Abbey, Dumfries-shire, 1703. [NAS.CH1.2.5.1]

MAXWELL, THOMAS, a student at Douai, 1771. [RSC.I.94]

MAXWELL, WILLIAM, son of James Maxwell of Kirkconnell, a student at the Scots College at Douai, 1691. [RSC.I.60]

MAXWELL, WILLIAM, born 1683, son of John Maxwell of Barncleugh, a student at the Scots College at Douai, 1698. [RSC.I.65]

MAXWELL, WILLIAM, Earl of Nithsdale, in Terregles, Dumfries-shire, 1703. [NAS.CH1.2.5.1]

MAXWELL, WILLIAM, in Drimly of Kirkconnel, New Abbey, Dumfries-shire, 1703. [NAS.CH1.2.5.1]

MAXWELL, WILLIAM, a barber in Dumfries, and his wife ....More, 1704. [NAS.CH1.5.2]

MAXWELL, WILLIAM, born 12 August 1745, son of Frederick Maxwell and Janet Harris, a student at Douai, 1756. [RSC.I.90]

MAXWELL, WILLIAM, a student at Douai, 1771. [RSC.I.94]

MAXWELL, ..., spouse to John Maxwell of Baltersan, Holywood, Dumfries-shire, 1705. [NAS.CH1.2.5.1]

MEEK, MARGARET, spouse to John Smellie an indweller in the Canongait, 'a papist' in Canongait, Edinburgh, 1703/1704/1705. [NAS.CH1.2.5.2.149/151/170]

MELDRUM, HELEN, in Robestoun, Kinnoir parish, 1710. [NAS.CH1.2.29.3/210]

MELLICE, ELSPET, in Bayrs, Parish of Bellie, 1710. [NAS.CH1.2.29.3/211]

MELVIN, WALTER, a servant at Traquair, Peebles-shire, 1705. [NAS.CH1.2.5.3/176]

MENZIES, ALEXANDER, born 1723, brother of the laird of Pitfoddels, at Ratisbon Seminary in 1735. [RSC.I.251]

MENZIES, or OGILVY, ANNA, a 'papist' in Liberton, Edinburgh, 1704. [NAS.CH1.2.5.2.149]

MENZIES, ANNA, born about 1645, 'in Carnwath's family', in Dalkeith, Midlothian,1705. [NAS.CH1.2.5/3]

MENZIES, DAVID, son of the laird of Pitfoddels, at Ratisbon Seminary, 1719. [SIG#294]

MENZIES, DAVID, born 1722, at Ratisbon Seminary 1735. [RSC.I.251]

MENZIES, DAVID, of Blairs, and Mrs Henrietta Gordon, a marriage contract, 1761. [SCA.FL3/1/3]

MENZIES, GILBERT, of Pitfoddels, Kincardineshire, 1705. [NAS.CH1.2.5.2]

MENZIES, JAMES, born 1689, son of Gilbert Menzies of Pitfodels, a student at the Scots College at Douai, 1700 to 1707. [RSC.I.65]

MENZIES, JAMES, and his wife Marjory Cumin, in Achnakyle, Strathaven, Banffshire, 1708. [NAS.CH1.2.30/1/28]

MENZIES, JAMES, at Ratisbon Seminary 1719. [SIG#294]

MENZIES, JAMES, at Ratisbon Seminary 1735. [SIG#294]

MENZIES, JEAN, daughter of the late Robert Menzies and his wife Jean Wachop in the Mill of Gilcomston, was baptised in Aberdeen by Father Robert Francis on 18 January 1698. [SNQ.VIII.182]

MENZIES, JOHN, at Ratisbon Seminary 1742. [SIG#294]

MENZIES, JOHN, of Pitfoddels, born 15 August 1756, son of John Menzies of Pitfoddels and Marianna Maxwell of Kirkconnell, a student at Douai, 1767. [RSC.I.93]

MENZIES, MARGARET, daughter of the late Robert Menzies in Mill of Gelcomston, a Protestant, and his wife Jean Wauchop, who was baptised as a Protestant when an infant, was baptised by on 29 September 1697 by Father Robert Francis. [SNQ.VIII.182]

MENZIES, MARJORY, daughter of the late Robert Menzies and his wife Jean Wachop in the Mill of Gilcomston, was baptised in Aberdeen by Father Robert Francis on 18 January 1698. [SNQ.VIII.182]

MENZIES, ROBERT, ordained at Douai before 1775, priest to the Highlanders in Edinburgh at Blackfriars Wynd until his death on 29 October 1791. [IR.XVIII.153]

MENZIES, WILLIAM, born 1688, eldest son of Gilbert Menzies of Pitfodels, a student at the Scots College at Douai, 1700-1707. [RSC.I.65]

MENZIES, WILLIAM, son of the laird of Pitfoddels, at Ratisbon Seminary 1719. [SIG#294]

MENZIES, WILLIAM, born 1721, at Ratisbon Seminary 1735. [RSC.I.251]

MENZIES, WILLIAM, of Pitfoddels, papers, 1755-1769. [SCA.FL3/1/4]

MICHIE, ALEXANDER, in the Muir of Glengarden, Aberdeenshire, 1718. [NAS.CH1.2.47.271]

MICHY, ALEXANDER, in Alnach, and his wife, in Glengarden, Aberdeenshire, 1718. [NAS.CH1.2.47.271]

MICHY, ALEXANDER, the elder, Alexander Michy the younger, and his wife Sarah Michy, in Foran, Glengarden, Aberdeenshire, 1718. [NAS.CH1.2.47.271]

MICHY, FINLAY, in Tullich, Glengarden, Aberdeenshire, 1718. [NAS.CH1.2.47.271]

MICHIE, JAMES, in Rinabouagh, with his wife Barbara Young and three children, in Forme, in Glenmuick, Tullich, and Glengarden, Aberdeenshire, 1718. [NAS.CH1.2.47/284]

MICHIE, JOHN, with his wife Katrine, and children John and Will, in the Muir of Glengarden, Aberdeenshire, 1718. [NAS.CH1.2.47.271]

MICHY, JOHN, and his wife in Alnach, in Glengarden, Aberdeenshire, 1718. [NAS.CH1.2.47.271]

MICHY, JOHN, a tailor in Alnach, in Glengarden, Aberdeenshire, 1718. [NAS.CH1.2.47.271]

MICHY, MARGERY, wife to Charles Taus, in Ardach, in Glenmuick, Tullich, and Glengarden, Aberdeenshire, 1718. [NAS.CH1.2.47/284]

MICHY, WILLIAM, and his wife in Alnach, Glengarden, Aberdeenshire, 1718. [NAS.CH1.2.47.271]

MILL, AGNES, daughter of John Mill and his wife Margaret Hall in the parish of St Machar, Aberdeen, was baptised as a Protestant when an infant, baptised by Father Robert Francis on 29 September 1696. [SNQ.VIII.181]

MILL, JAMES, a tenant, with his wife Margaret Simson, and daughter Isobel, in Fochabers, 1710. [NAS.CH1.2.29.3/210]

MILL, JOHN, a tenant, with his wife Isobel Gordon, in Cottonhill, Parish of Bellie, 1710. [NAS.CH1.2.29.3/211]

MILL, THOMAS, tenant of Kyriggs, with his wife Isobel Gallan, parish of Bellie, 1710. [NAS.CH1.2.29.3]

MILLER, GEORGE, servant to Robert Corson, New Abbey, Dumfries-shire, 1703. [NAS.CH1.2.5.1]

MILLER, HUGH, and family, in Guisachan, Kiltarlity, Inverness-shire, 1710. [NAS.CH1.2.29.3]

MILLIGAN, JANET, in Terregles and Kirkgunzeon, Aberdeenshire, 1705. [NAS.CH1.2.5.2]

MILNE, MARGARET, spouse to William Bowman in Carnborrow, Glass, 1710. [NAS.CH1.2.29.3]

MITCHELL, AGNES, wife of James Mitchell, parish of Bellie, 1710. [NAS.CH1.2.29.3]

MITCHELL, AGNES, in Landends, Parish of Bellie, 1710. [NAS.CH1.2.29.3/211]

MITCHELL, ALEXANDER, a schoolmaster at Fochabers, Morayshire, 1720. [NLS.ms68.31-32]

MITCHELL, ANDREW, a chapman in parish of Bellie, 1710. [NAS.CH1.2.29.3]

MITCHELL, ANDREW, a tenant, with his wife Elspet Gallan, and daughters Agnes and Janet, Parish of Bellie, 1710. [NAS.CH1.2.29.3/211]

MITCHELL, CATHERINE, in Canongait, Edinburgh, 1703. [NAS.CH1.2.5.2/151]

MITCHELL, ELIZABETH, servant to Lady Largo, 'a papist' in the Abbey, Canongait, Edinburgh, 1703/1704/1705. [NAS.CH1.2.5.2.149/151/170]

MITCHELL, JAMES, 1714. [NLS.ms976.143]

MITCHELL, KATHERINE, a 'papist' in Canongait, Edinburgh, 1704. [NAS.CH1.2.5.2/149]

MITCHELL, MARJORY, born in Castle Gordon, parish of Belly, Banffshire, a spinner in the Musselburgh Woollen Manufactory, 'a papist' in Musselburgh, Edinburgh, 1705. [NAS.CH1.2.5.2.167]

MITCHELL, ISOBEL, in Fochabers, Morayshire, 1705. [NAS.CH1.2.5/2]

MITCHELL, JANET, in Fochabers, Morayshire, 1705. [NAS.CH1.2.5/2]

MITCHELL, MARY, a servant of Boynd, parish of Bellie, 1710. [NAS.CH1.2.29.3]

MITCHELL, PENELOPE, in Fochabers, Morayshire, 1705. [NAS.CH1.2.5/2]

MITCHELL, THOMAS, and his wife Janet Ross, in Bogtoun, Kinnoir parish, 1710. [NAS.CH1.2.29.3/210]

MITCHELL, WILLIAM, a servant at Burnside, parish of Bellie, 1710. [NAS.CH1.2.29.3]

MITCHELL, WILLIAM, tenant in Wallheads, with his wife Marjorie Cuie, and son John, parish of Bellie, 1710. [NAS.CH1.2.29.3]

MITCHELL, ..., a servant at Balnacraig, Aboyne or Glentanar, 1710. [NAS.CH1.2.29.3]

MITCHELSON, BESSIE, in Dalbeattie, Orr, Dumfries-shire, 1705. [NAS.CH1.2.5/156]

MOIR, MARGARET, in Fochabers, Morayshire, 1705. [NAS.CH1.2.5/2]

MONTEITH, MARY, a washer and a linen-dresser, residing in Orr's land, a 'papist' in Canongait, Edinburgh, 1703/1704. [NAS.CH1.2.5.2/149/151]

MOIR, JAMES, born 1761, at Ratisbon Seminary, 1772. [SIG.295][RSC.I.253]

MOIR, THOMAS, at Ratisbon Seminary, 1784. [SIG.295][RSC.I.254]

MORE, ISOBEL, a widow in Strathaven, Banffshire, 1708. [NAS.CH1.2.30/1/28]

MORE, MARY, in Bowhouse, Terregles, Dumfries-shire, 1703. [NAS.CH1.2.5.1]

MORE, WILLIAM, a carver, with his son William More, in College Kirk parish, Edinburgh, 1703. [NAS.CH1.2.5.2]

MORGAN, ANNA, aged 4 years, daughter of William Morgan a carver, residing with James Paterson a tailor in the Canongait, Edinburgh, 1704. [NAS.CH1.2.5.2/149]

MORGAN, DONALD BAIN, his wife Janet Morgan, and son John, in Foran, Glengarden, Aberdeenshire,1718. [NAS.CH1.2.47.271]

MORGAN, JANET, in Foran, Glengarden, Aberdeenshire, 1718. [NAS.CH1.2.47.271]

MORGAN, WILLIAM, a carter, his son William, and Francis ... his servant, in Edinburgh, 'papists' in College Kirk parish, Edinburgh, 1703/1704/ 1705. [NAS.CH1.2.5.2.149/151/171]

MORRIS, JAMES, a fencing master in Aberdeen, 1704/1705. [NAS.CH1.2.5.2/155]

MORRISON, ADAM, in Robestoun, Kinnoir parish, 1710. [NAS.CH1.2.29.3/210]

MORRISON, ADAM, and his wife Elspet Reid, at the Raws of Huntly, Dunbennan parish, 1710. [NAS.CH1.2.29.3/210]

MORRISON, ANNA, born 11 April 1690, daughter of Andrew Morrison in Quartans near Drum, Aberdeenshire, was baptised by Father Robert Francis on 13 April 1690. [SNQ.VIII.181]

MORRISON, AUGUSTUS, from the Diocese of Aberdeen, at the Monastry of Ratisbon from 1704 until his death in 1734. [SIG#293]

MORRISON, HELEN, a school-teacher in Culreach, Parish of Bellie, 1710. [NAS.CH1.2.29.3/211]

MORRISON, JANET, in Barnbarrach, Colvend, Dumfries-shire, 1704. [NAS.CH1.2.5.2]

MORRISON, JEAN, in Westertoun, Kinnoir parish, 1710. [NAS.CH1.2.29.3/210]

MORRISON, MARJORY, wife to James Robertson, in the parish of Bellie, 1710. [NAS.CH1.2.29.3/211]

MORRISON, PATRICK, a merchant in Aberdeen, and his son Patrick, Aberdeen, 1704/1705. [NAS.CH1.2.5.2/155]

MORRORE, KATHERINE, spouse to Frederick Maxwell in Barnbackie, Lochrutton, Dumfries-shire, 1703. [NAS.CH1.2.5.1]

MORTIMER, ELSPET, a servant in Nether Badfeure, parish of Bellie, 1710. [NAS.CH1.2.29.3]

MORTIMER, JAMES, a tenant in Upper Achinroth, with his wife Barbara Johnstoun, in the parish of Bellie, 1710. [NAS.CH1.2.29.3/211]

MORTIMER, JAMES, in Parish of Bellie, 1710. [NAS.CH1.2.29.3/211]

MORTIMER, Mrs MARY, in Soutrolcroft, Banffshire. 1794. [NAS.SC2.72.4]

MUIRHEAD, GAVIN, of Lauchop, parish of Bothwell, 'a papist', 1683. [RPCS.VIII.646]

MULLIGAN, AGNES, in Terregles, Dumfries-shire, 1703. [NAS.CH1.2.5.1]

MULLIGAN, ANNA, in Terregles, Dumfries-shire, 1703. [NAS.CH1.2.5.1]

MULLIGAN, JAN, in Terregles, Dumfries-shire, 1703. [NAS.CH1.2.5.1]

MULLIGAN, JANET, spouse to John Ridge in Kirkconnel, Dumfries-shire, 1703. [NAS.CH1.2.5.1]

MUNRO, GEORGE, an apostate in Comar, Kiltarlity, 1679. [IR.XXIV.82]

MUNRO, ROBERT, born 1646, an apostate, educated at Douai from 1663 priest in Strathglass from the 1670s, died in Glengarry Castle on 17 January 1704. [IR.XXIV.76-78; LV.206]

MURRAY, AGNES, daughter of the late James Murray, a Protestant and a merchant in Turriff, Aberdeenshire, and Agnes Cuming his wife, aCtholic, (now wife to Thomas Russell in Elgin, who was baptised as a Protestant when an infant, was baptised by on 29 September 1697 by Father Robert Francis. [SNQ.VIII.182]

MURRAY, FRANCIS, a priest in Dumfries, Galloway, and Tweeddale, 1714. [NLS.ms976.143]

MURRAY, HELEN, daughter of old Lady Conhaith, in Holywood, Dumfries-shire, 1705. [NAS.CH1.2.5.1]

MURRAY, JAMES, of Punheath (?), with his wife Agnes Glendinning, in Parton, Kirkcudbrightshire, 1705. [NAS.CH1.2.5.2]

MURRAY, JAMES, a flaxdresser in Keith, Banffshire, 1794. [NAS.SC2.72.4]

MURRAY, LUCIE, daughter of old Lady Conhaith, in Holywood, Dumfries-shire, 1705. [NAS.CH1.2.5.1]

son in Pasley's Close, Edinburgh, ' papists' in College Kirk parish, Edinburgh, 1703/1705. [NAS.CH1.2.5.2.151/175/1]

MURRAY, MARGARET, in Ruthven, Strathbogie,1710. [NAS.CH1.2.29.3/209]

MURRAY, MARY, in Ruthven, Strathbogie,1710. [NAS.CH1.2.29.3/209]

NAIRNE, ANN, a chambermaid at Traquair, Peebles-shire, 1705. [NAS.CH1.2.5.3/176]

NAIRN, JOHN, son of Major David Nairn and .... Murray, a student at Douai, 1742. [RSC.I.85]

NAPIER, ..., of Wrightshouses, West Kirk parish, Edinburgh, 'a papist', 1681. [RPCS.VII.728]

NEILSON, ROBERT, the younger of Barnkyllie, aged above 20 years, and his wife Elizabeth Stewart, also his sister, in Kirkpatrick-Durham, Dumfries-shire, 1703. [NAS.CH1.2.5.1]

NICOLSON, JEAN, at the Raws of Huntly, Dunbennan parish, 1710. [NAS.CH1.2.29.3/210]

NICOLSON, NIGEL, born 1664, a student at the Scots College at Douai, 1687. [RSC.I.56]

NICOLSON, THOMAS, born Birkenbog, Banffshire, 1648, son of Thomas Nicolson and Elizabeth Abercromby, educated at the Scots College at Douai, 1682, ordained in Padua, 1686, Vicar Apostolic of Scotland from 1695, died at Preshome on 12 October 1718. [CDS][RSC.I.56]

NICOLSON, ..., a priest in Aberdeen, 1714. [NLS.ms976.143]

NICOLSON, THOMAS, born 1741, a student at Douai, 1751. [RSC.I.88]

NICOLSON, WILLIAM, son of James Nicolson and Joan Kernighen, a student at Douai, 1749. [RSC.I.87]

NIDDRIE, the laird of, and his wife, apostates and 'papists' in Liberton, Edinburgh, apostates and 'papists', 1704. [NAS.CH1.2.5.2.149]

NILSON, ROBERT, of Barnkoily, a student at the Scots College at Douai, 1699. [RSC.I.65]

NINIAN, PATRICK, born 1673, from Wemyss, son of James Ninian, a student at the Scots College at Douai, 1695. [RSC.I.64]

NODAM, Mrs, in Fochabers, 1710. [NAS.CH1.2.29.3/210]

NORIE, WILLIAM, with his daughters Jean and Helen, in Haddoch, Ruthven, Strathbogie, 1710. [NAS.CH1.2.29.3/209]

NORIE, WILLIAM, and his spouse Isobel Cruickshank, in Milne of Kinnoir, Kinnoir parish, 1710. [NAS.CH1.2.29.3/210]

OCHTERLONY, Miss BETTY, died in Dundee on 12 April 1782. [IR.XVII.46/77]

ODIE, JOHN IGNATIUS, born 1699, a student at the Scots College in Madrid, 1710. [RSC.I.199]

OGG, MARGARET, an old woman in Kinnoir parish, 1710. [NAS.CH1.2.29.3/210]

OGILVIE, ELIZABETH, governess to Lady Mary Keith, in Edinburgh, 1704. [NAS.CH1.2.5.2]

OGILVIE, GEORGE, in Drummure, Botriphnie, 1710. [NAS.CH1.2.29.3/209]

OGILVIE, ISOBEL, a wardrobe servant at Traquair, Peebles-shire, 1705. [NAS.CH1.2.5.3/176]

OGILVIE, ISIDORE, born 1670, at Wurzburg in 1693, ordained in 1694, died 1701. [SF.272/281]

OGILVIE, JEAN, a shopkeeper in Edinburgh, 'a papist' residing in Captain Moncreiff's land in Forrester's Wynd, New North Kirk parish, Edinburgh, 1704/1705. [NAS.CH1.2.5.2.149/154/175/1]

OGILVIE, JEAN, daughter of the late Provost of Banff, lodging below Mrs Nicols, 'a papist' in New Kirk parish, Edinburgh, 1705. [NAS.CH1.2.5.2.175/1]

OGILVIE, JOHN, the younger a servant in Foran, Glengarden, Aberdeenshire, 1718. [NAS.CH1.2.47.271]

OGILVIE, MARGARET, 'a papist' in Canongait parish, Edinburgh, 1705. [NAS.CH1.2.5.2.170]

OGILVIE, MARY, daughter of the late Provost of Banff, lodging below Mrs Nicols, 'a papist' in New Kirk parish, Edinburgh, 1705. [NAS.CH1.2.5.2.175/1]

OGILVIE, THOMAS JOSEPH, a lay-brother of Ratisbon Monastery, 1684. [SF#281]

OGILVIE, ..., servant or gentlewoman to Mary Byars in Edinburgh, 'a papist' in Tron Kirk parish, Edinburgh, 1704/ 1705. [NAS.CH1.2.5.2.149; 175/1]

OGILVY, HENRY, a student at the Scots College in Valladolid, 1770, died 14 September 1773. [RSC.I.204]

OIG, ALEXANDER, and family, in Kirkton of Comar, Kiltarlity, Inverness-shire, 1710. [NAS.CH1.2.29.3]

OLIPHANT, ELIZABETH, at the Raws of Huntly, Dunbennan parish, 1710. [NAS.CH1.2.29.3/210]

O'NEIL, ALEXANDER, a priest at Inverness Castle, 1681. [IR.XXIV.82]

PACKMAN, JAMES, tenant in Nether Dallachie, with his wife Catherine Weir, and children Bessie and Isobel, in the parish of Bellie, 1710. [NAS.CH1.2.29.3/211]

PACKSTON, ELSPET, at the Raws of Huntly, Dunbennan parish, 1710. [NAS.CH1.2.29.3/210]

PAIN, HENRY NEVILLE, a priest captured in Annandale and imprisoned in Edinburgh Castle, 1690. [RPCS.XV.274]

PAIN, JOHN, in College, Terregles, Dumfries-shire, 1703. [NAS.CH1.2.5.1]

PAIN, JOHN, in Lincluden, Dumfries-shire, 1703. [NAS.CH1.2.5.1]

PAIN, JOHN, 'a papist' in Linton, 1705. [NAS.CH1.2.5.2.172]

PAIT, JOHN, and his spouse Agnes Davidson, also daughters Janet and Mary, in Dalbeattie, Orr, Dumfries-shire, 1705. [NAS.CH1.2.5/156]

PANTON, ANNA, daughter of Hendrie Panton of Hiltoun and his wife Ann Irvin in the parish of St Nicolas, Aberdeen, was baptised as a Protestant when an infant, later baptised by Father Robert Francis on 29 September 1696. [SNQ.VIII.181]

PANTON, JAMES, son of Hendrie Panton of Hilton, was baptised as a Protestant when young, baptised as a Catholic by Father Robert Francis in Aberdeen on 18 January 1698. [SNQ.VIII.182]

PANTON, JEREMY, from Aberdeen, at Ratisbon Monastery 1687, died 1719. [SIG#293]

PANTON, WILLIAM, in Ruthven, Strathbogie,1710. [NAS.CH1.2.29.3/209]

PARNAN, DAVID, son of Andrew Parnan, in Richorne, Orr, Dumfries-shire, 1705. [NAS.CH1.2.5/156]

PARNAN, ROBERT, and his spouse Janet Williamson, in Richorne, Orr, Dumfries-shire, 1705. [NAS.CH1.2.5/156]

PATERSON, AGNES, wife to Alexander Steinson, in Coldham, Parish of Bellie, 1710. [NAS.CH1.2.29.3/211]

PATERSON, ALEXANDER, a tenant, with his wife Isobel Anderson, parish of Bellie, 1710. [NAS.CH1.2.29.3]

PATERSON, ALEXANDER, born 1686 in Tynet, schoolmaster at Morar, ordained in Paris during 1715, a priest in Uist later in Strathbogie and Huntly by 1735, died 1747 in Huntly, Aberdeenshire. [IR.XVIII.133]

PATERSON, ALEXANDER, master of the Scots College at Douai in 1793, later Vicar Apostolic of the Lowlands District. [IR.LVIII.223]

PATERSON, BARBARA, born about 1690, servant in Fetteresso, Kincardineshire, 1704. [NAS.CH1.2.5.3/201]

PATERSON, ELSPET, wife of William Dunbar, in Fochabers, 1710. [NAS.CH1.2.29.3/210]

PATERSON, JAMES, of Woodside, parish of Dalserf, 'a papist', 1683. [RPCS.VIII.650]

PATERSON, JAMES, a tailor in the Canongait, and his spouse Alison Graham, also their daughter Barbara, 'papists' in Canongait parish, Edinburgh, 1704/1705. [NAS.CH1.2.5.2.149/154/170]

PATERSON, JAMES, son of Alexander Paterson, in Dryburn, parish of Bellie, 1710. [NAS.CH1.2.29.3]

PATERSON, JAMES, a student at the Scots College at Douai, 1793. [IR.LVIII.223]

PATERSON, JOHN, tenant of the laird of Kirkconnel, his wife Agnes Wright and his daughter Nicola aged 14, New Abbey, Dumfries-shire, 1703. [NAS.CH1.2.5.1]

PATERSON, MARJORIE, wife of William Forbes a tenant, and their daughter Margaret Forbes, in Fochabers, Morayshire, 1705; also daughter Margaret, in Fochabers, 1710. [NAS.CH1.2.5/2, 187; 2.29.3/210]

PATERSON, ROBERT, in Woodhead, Terregles, Dumfries-shire, 1703. [NAS.CH1.2.5.1]

PATON, JOHN, a tenant in Dilvan, with his wife Isobel Thomson, and children Robert aged 14, Janet aged 13, John aged 10, and a recently baptised child, in Kelton, Kirkcudbrightshire, 1705. [NAS.CH1.2.5.2]

PAUL, Madam, a housekeeper at Gordon Castle, Morayshire, 1705. [NAS.CH1.2.5/187]

PEARSON, AGNES, in Barnbarrach, Colvend, Dumfries-shire, 1704. [NAS.CH1.2.5.2]

PEARSON, ANDREW, in Barnbarrach, Colvend, Dumfries-shire, 1704. [NAS.CH1.2.5.2]

PENMAN, MARIE, a servant to Lady Pitfodell, in College Kirk parish, Edinburgh, 1703. [NAS.CH1.2.5.2/151]

PEPPER, CHARLES, from Crieff, educated at Douai 1747, in St Andrews by 1782. [IR.XVII.77][RSC.I.86]

PEPPER, JOHN, from Crieff, educated at Douai

PEPPER, JOHN, from Crieff, educated at Douai, a Jesuit and chaplain at Terregles, 17..... [IR.XVII.78][RSC.I.93]

PEPPER, WILLIAM 'KILIAN', born Crieff in 1738, educated at Douai from 1749, ordained at Wurzburg, to Scotland in 1784, chaplain to the Leslies of Fetternear, later in Dundee. [IR.XVII.78][RSC.I.87]

PETER, JOHN, his wife Margaret Richie, and 3 children, in Tomnafiagh, Glengarden, Aberdeenshire, 1718. [NAS.CH1.2.47.271]

PETERSON, ALEXANDER, 'excomm.', in Tullich, Glengarden, Aberdeenshire, 1718. [NAS.CH1.2.47.271]

PETRIE, ANN, a servant at Traquair, Peebles-shire, 1705. [NAS.CH1.2.5.3/176]

PETRIE, JAMES, at the Bridgend of Banff, Banffshire, 1794. [NAS.SC2.72.4]

PETRIE, JOHN, a waulker in Innerleithen, and his spouse Ann Robb, Peebles-shire, 1705. [NAS.CH1.2.5.3/176]

PIRNIE, JOHN, a mason in Kirkton of Cargill, Perthshire, with his sons James and Edward, 1704. [NAS.CH1.2.5.3.203]

PITCAIRN, HENRY, of Pitlour, an apostate in South Leith, Edinburgh, 1703. [NAS.CH1.2.5.2/151]

PITCAIRN, JOHN, late of Pitlour, 'apostatized in King James's reign', residing at the head of Rotten Row, South Leith, a 'papist', 1704. [NAS.CH1.2.5.2.149]

PITFODDELS, Lady, in Aberdeenshire, 1714. [NLS.ms976.143]

PONTON, THOMAS, a smith, and his wife Katherine NcEntire, Strathaven, Banffshire, 1708. [NAS.CH1.2.30/1/28]

PORTER, GEORGE, a cottar in Munches, with his wife Elizabeth Wilson, and children Janet, Alexander, and John, Kirkcudbrightshire, 1705.[NAS.CH1.2.5.2]

PORTERFIELD, ..., Lady Comistoun, and her children Walter and Jean, residing at the foot of Bell's Wynd, Old Kirk parish, Edinburgh, 1704. Walter Porterfield a surgeon and the laird of Dirleton are their nearest Protestant relations. [NAS.CH1.2.5.2/149]

PORTERFIELD, JEAN, in Edinburgh, 'a papist' in Old Kirk parish, Edinburgh, 1705. [NAS.CH1.2.5.2.175/1]

PORTERFIELD, WALTER, in Edinburgh, 'a papist' in Tron Kirk parish, Edinburgh, 1705. [NAS.CH1.2.5.2.175/1]

PRIESTLY, JAMES, a servant in Upper Dallachie, Parish of Bellie, 1710. [NAS.CH1.2.29.3/211]

PRIMROSE, PATRICK, a priest in Aberchirder, Banffshire, 1670, imprisoned in Banff Tolbooth, banished from Scotland, but died in Botriphnie in 1671. [IR.XXIII.59]

PRINGLE, ..., sometime laird of Graycrook, a 'papist', residing with James Clerk of Wrightshouses, in West Kirk parish, Edinburgh, 1704. [NAS.CH1.2.5.2.149]

PYRIE, HENDRIE, and his wife Jean Coupar, at the Boat of Kinnoir parish, 1710. [NAS.CH1.2.29.3/210]

PYRIE, JOHN, in Gibstoun, Kinnoir parish, 1710. [NAS.CH1.2.29.3/210]

RANKINE, JAMES, a merchant in Fochabers, his wife Barbara Ritchie, and children John, George, and Margaret, Morayshire, 1705; with children John, Alexander, and Margaret, in Bellie, 1710. [NAS.CH1.2.5/2;CH1.2.29.3]

RATCLIFFE, HENRY, page to Lady Kilsyth, 1705. [NAS.CH1.2.5.3]

RATCLIFFE, ISOBEL, servant to the Kilsyth family in Glasgow, 1703. [NAS.CH1.2.5.1]

RATHVEN, WILLIAM, a servant in the parish of Bellie, 1710. [NAS.CH1.2.29.3]

RATTRAY, WILLIAM, a convert from Coupar Angus, formerly an apprentice saddler in Dunkeld, a student at the Scots College in Valladolid, 1785, ordained there, a priest in Scotland fron 1796. At Strathbogie, Stobhall and Dundee, died there 2 February 1827. [IR.XVII.84][RSC.I.209]

REID, ALEXANDER, servant to Robert Brown of Bishopton, 'suspected to be Popish', in Kirkmahoe, Dumfries-shire, 1704. [NAS.CH1.2.5.2]

REID, ALEXANDER, tenant in Cowie Muir, and his wife Margaret Smith, in the parish of Bellie, 1710. [NAS.CH1.2.29.3/211]

REID, ALEXANDER, a servant of Boynd, parish of Bellie, 1710. [NAS.CH1.2.29.3]

REID, ALEXANDER, a servant in Tullo, Parish of Bellie, 1710. [NAS.CH1.2.29.3/211]

REID, ALEXANDER, servant in Tullo, Parish of Bellie, 1710. [NAS.CH1.2.29.3/211]

REID, ALEXANDER, a student at the Scots College at Valladolid, 1771, died in April 1774. [RSC.I.205]

REID, ALEXANDER, at Ratisbon Seminary, 1788. [RSC.I.254][SIG#295]

REID, BESSIE, wife to Andrew Gray tenant in Nether Achinroth, in the parish of Bellie, 1710. [NAS.CH1.2.29.3/211]

REID, BETTIE, parish of Bellie, 1710. [NAS.CH1.2.29.3]

REID, EPHRAIM, from Tain, Ross and Cromarty, at Ratisbon Monastery 1663, died 1712. [SIG#293]

REID, ISABEL, in the parish of Bellie, 1710. [NAS.CH1.2.29.3/211]

REID, JANE, a servant in the parish of Bellie, 1710. [NAS.CH1.2.29.3]

REID, JANET, wife of John Bartlet, in Ruthven, Strathbogie,1710. [NAS.CH1.2.29.3/209]

REID, JEAN, spouse to Edmond Reid a hoy boy, in Tron Kirk parish, Edinburgh, 1703. [NAS.CH1.2.5.2/151]

REID, JEAN, in Kyriggs, parish of Bellie, 1710. [NAS.CH1.2.29.3]

REID, MARGARET, spouse to Arthur Watson late soldier in Edinburgh Castle, 'apostatized about twenty years ago', a 'papist' living in Restalrig, South Leith , Edinburgh, 1704. [NAS.CH1.2.5.2.149]

REID, MARGARET, 'wife to the under-cook', in Fochabers, 1710. [NAS.CH1.2.29.3/210]

REID, MARJORIE, born in Castle Gordon, parish of Belly, Banffshire, a spinner in the Musselburgh Woollen Manufactory, 'a papist' in Musselburgh, Edinburgh, 1705. [NAS.CH1.2.5.2/167; 3/182]

REID, MARJORY, in Fochabers, 1710. [NAS.CH1.2.29.3/210]

REID, PETER, son of Alexander Reid and Isabella Blebars in the diocese of Brechin, educated at the Scots College in Paris in 1701, ordained in Rome in 1706, died at Preshome on 27 November 1726. [SCP#213]

REID, THOMAS, and Isabel, servants in the parish of Bellie, 1710. [NAS.CH1.2.29.3]

REID, WILLIAM, a suspected priest who had returned to Scotland, was imprisoned in Aberdeen Tolbooth in 1690. [RPCS.XVI.469]

REID, WILLIAM, ordained in Rome by 1739, then a missionary at Mortlach for about 30 years, died in Aberdeen on 26 March 1785. [IR.XVII.53]

REID, WILLIAM, priest in Kempcairn, Banffshire, 1794. [NAS.SC2.72.4]

RENDAL, ELIZABETH, the Duchess of Gordon's gentlewoman, a 'papist' in the Canongait, Edinburgh, 1704. [NAS.CH1.2.5.2/149]

RENDAL, JANET, in Colvend, Dumfries-shire, 1704. [NAS.CH1.2.5.2]

RIACH, ALEXANDER, and his wife Anna Farquharson, in Strathaven, Banffshire, 1708. [NAS.CH1.2.30/1/28]

RIACH, ELSPET, a widow in Foderlaitter, Strathaven, Banffshire, 1708. [NAS.CH1.2.30/1/28]

RIACH, GEORGE, in Miln of Arbrek, Botriphnie, 1710. [NAS.CH1.2.29.3]

RIACH, JAMES, a merchant in Strathaven, Banffshire, 1708. [NAS.CH1.2.30/1/28]

RIACH, JOHN, in Foderlaitter, Strathaven, Banffshire, 1708. [NAS.CH1.2.30/1/28]

RICHARDSON, ALEXANDER, in Ruthven, Strathbogie,1710. [NAS.CH1.2.29.3/209]

RICHIE, CALUM, with his wife Isobel McAndrew, and two children, in Lairy, Glenmuick, Tullich, and Glengarden, Aberdeenshire, 1718. [NAS.CH1.2.47/284]

RICHIE, JANET, a servant in Rothiemay, Strathbogie, 1710. [NAS.CH1.2.29.3]

RICHIE, JANET, wife of Andrew Hossack at the Milne of Fochabers, 1710. [NAS.CH1.2.29.3]

RICHIE, JOHN, with his spouse Isobel Michy, his son John and three daughters, in Glenmuick, Tullich, and Glengarden, Aberdeenshire, 1718. [NAS.CH1.2.47/284]

RICHIE, WILLIAM, a fisher in Campsie, Cargill, Perthshire, and his wife Anne Hay a schoolmistress, 1704. [NAS.CH1.2.5.3.203]

RIDDOCH, ALEXANDER, in Oldtoun of Drumgask, Aboyne or Glentanar, Aberdeenshire, 1704, 1710. [NAS.CH1.2.5/190; CH1.2.29/3]

RIDDOCH, JOHN, a writer, and his spouse Anna Hepburn, in Edinburgh, and their children John and William, apostates and 'papists' in Cross Close, Old Kirk parish, Edinburgh,1703/ 1704/1705. Mr George Jollie's widow is his nearest Protestant kin while a Mr Stark is her nearest. [NAS.CH1.2.5.2.149/151; 175/1]

RIDDOCH, JOHN, rector of the Scots College at Douai, 27 August 1743, 17 January 1757. [RSC.I.85/90]

RIDDOCH, WILLIAM, tacksman in Garrichow, Comrie, Perthshire, under Lord Drummond, and his children, 1703. [NAS.CH1.2.5.2]

RIDGE, JAMES, tenant in Greenmerse, his daughters Marion aged 12, Agnes aged 8, Elizabeth aged 10, Nicola aged 2, sons George aged 6, James aged 12, John aged 16, New Abbey, Dumfries-shire, 1703. [NAS.CH1.2.5.1]

RIDGE, JAMES, tenant or cottar in Cargan, with his wife Janet Wright, and children Clement, James, Janet, and John, in Traquair, Dumfries-shire, 1703. [NAS.CH1.2.5.1]

RIDGE, JANET, spouse to William Fleming in Kirkconnel, Dumfries-shire, 1703. [NAS.CH1.2.5.1]

RIDGE, JEAN, in Kirkconnel, Dumfries-shire, 1703. [NAS.CH1.2.5.1]

RIDGE, JOHN, tenant in Townhead of Kirkconnel, and his wife Marion McNoe, daughters Agnes aged 4, Elizabeth, Janet aged 15, Jean aged 1,Marion aged 12, sons James aged 6, in Dumfries-shire, 1703. [NAS.CH1.2.5.1]

RIDGE, JOHN, the elder, tenant in Townhead of Kirkconnel, and daughter Katherine, in New Abbey, Dumfries-shire, 1703. [NAS.CH1.2.5.1]

RIDGE, NICOLA, mother to James Ridge in Townhead of Kirkconnel, Dumfries-shire, 1703. [NAS.CH1.2.5.1]

RIGG, AGNES, wife of John Jamieson in Bankend, Caerlaverock, Dumfries-shire, 1704. [NAS.CH1.2.5.2]

RIGG, DAVID, and his spouse Katherine Carruthers, in Mabie, Troquair, Orr, Dumfries-shire, 1705. [NAS.CH1.2.5/156]

RIGG, ELSPETH, servant to William Fleming in Buss of Kirkconnel, New Abbey, Dumfries-shire, 1703. [NAS.CH1.2.5.1]

RIGG, JAMES, and his wife Janet Wright, sons – Robert, John, William, and Clement, also a daughter, in Troquair, Orr, Dumfries-shire, 1705. [NAS.CH1.2.5/156]

RIGG, JANET, in Troquair, Orr, Dumfries-shire, 1703, 1705. [NAS.CH1.2.5.1/156]

RIGG, JOHN, and children John, and Marion, in Mabie, Troquair, Orr, Dumfries-shire, 1703, 1705. [NAS.CH1.2.5.1/156]

RIGG, MARION, in Buss of Kirkconnel, New Abbey, Dumfries-shire, 1703. [NAS.CH1.2.5.1]

RIGG, MARION, widow of John Wright, in Traquair, Dumfries-shire, 1703. [NAS.CH1.2.5.1]

RIND, ELSPETH, spouse to James Mitchell a brewer in Fochabers, Morayshire, 1705. [NAS.CH1.2.5/2, 187]

RIND, MARGARET, in Fochabers, Morayshire, 1705. [NAS.CH1.2.5/2]

RITCHIE, WILLIAM, a fisher in Campsie, and his wife Anne Hay a schoolmistress, Cargill, Perthshire, 1703. [NAS.CH1.2.5.2]

ROBB, JAMES, a student at the Scots College at Valladolid, 1780. [RSC.I.209]

ROBERT, ISOBEL, daughter of ....Robert, a tailor, in the parish of St Machar, Aberdeen, was baptised as a Protestant when an infant, later baptised by Father Robert Francis on 29 September 1696. [SNQ.VIII.181]

ROBERTSON, ALEXANDER, a farmer in Fochabers, with children James and Katherine, Morayshire, 1705, 1710. [NAS.CH1.2.5/2; 2.29.3/210]

ROBERTSON, ALEXANDER, a workman, and his children James and Katherine, in Fochabers, Morayshire, 1705. [NAS.CH1.2.5/2, 187]

ROBERTSON, ALEXANDER, a servant in Althash, parish of Bellie, 1710. [NAS.CH1.2.29.3]

ROBERTSON, BESSIE, a servant in the Parish of Bellie, 1710. [NAS.CH1.2.29.3/211]

ROBERTSON, CHARLES, born 1753, son of Isaac Robertson and Anna Cattenach, a student at Douai, 1766, 1771. [RSC.I.93/94]

ROBERTSON, DONALD, sometime of Nathro, now in Gateside, an inn-keeper, 'a papist' in Angus, 1704, 1705. [NAS.CH1.2.5.3.204; CH1.2.5.2.171]

ROBERTSON, JAMES, a servant to John Robertson a merchant in Fochabers, Morayshire, 1705. [NAS.CH1.2.5/2, 187]

ROBERTSON, JAMES, born 1758, a student at Douai in 1771, at Ratisbon Seminary in 1772, ordained in 1782, died 1820. [SIG#295][RSC.I.253]; probate 16 Dec.1820.[NA.Prob.11/637]

ROBERTSON, JANET, in the parish of Bellie, 1710. [NAS.CH1.2.29.3/211]

ROBERTSON, JOHN, in Waterside of Kincardine, Aboyne or Glentanar, Aberdeenshire, 1704. [NAS.CH1.2.5/190]

ROBERTSON, MARGARET, wife to John Christy, in Cottonhill, Parish of Bellie, 1710. [NAS.CH1.2.29.3/211]

ROBERTSON, WILLIAM, a servant in Dryburn, parish of Bellie, 1710. [NAS.CH1.2.29.3]

ROBSON, MARGARET or MARY, in Green Milne, Caerlaverock, Dumfries, 1705. [NAS.CH1.2.5.1]

RODDAN, DOUGALD, tenant of the laird of Kirkconnel, and his wife Elizabeth Smart, also daughter Janet, in New Abbey, Dumfries-shire, 1703. [NAS.CH1.2.5.1]

RODDICK, BARBARA, and her mother ..... Maxwell, in Green Milne, Caerlaverock, Dumfries-shire, 1705. [NAS.CH1.2.5.1]

ROLLAND, JOSEPH, at Ratisbon Monastery, 1734. [SIG#294]

ROLLAND, WILLIAM, at Ratisbon Monastery, 1772. [SIG#295][RSC.I.253]

ROMMIE, ANDREW, tenant in Wallheads, with Marjory Mitchell his wife, parish of Bellie, 1710. [NAS.CH1.2.29.3]

ROSE, MARGARET, a widow in Ruthven, Strathbogie,1710. [NAS.CH1.2.29.3/209]

ROSLYNN, Lady, in College Kirk parish, Edinburgh, 1703. [NAS.CH1.2.5.2]

ROSS, ALEXANDER, born 1750, son of Robert Ross and Marie Stuart, a student at Douai, 1761. [RSC.I.92]

ROSS, AMBROSE, from Ross-shire, at Ratisbon Monastery 1708, died 1714. [SIG#293]

ROY, CHARLES, at Ratisbon Seminary, 1772. [SIG#295][RSC.I.253]

RUDDACH, ISOBEL, in Ruthven, Strathbogie, 1710. [NAS.CH1.2.29.3/209]

RUNSIMAN, MARGARET, in Cumry, in Ruthven, Strathbogie,1710. [NAS.CH1.2.29.3/209]

RUSSELL, ALEXANDER, born 1667, son of William Russell, a Writer to the Signet, and Catherine Leslie of Tulloch, a student at the Scots College at Douai, 1688. [RSC.I.60]

RUSSELL, ALEXANDER, tenant in Nether Dallachie, with his wife Isobel Forsyth, and son John, in the parish of Bellie, 1710. [NAS.CH1.2.29.3/211]

RYAN, HUGH, to Scotland in 1681, a priest and physician in Chisholm's country, Inverness-shire, 1670s. [IR.XXIV.83]

RYND, LILIAS, at the Raws of Huntly, Dunbennan parish, 1710. [NAS.CH1.2.29.3/210]

ST COLM, PETER, a musician in Edinburgh, 'a papist' in Tron Kirk parish, Edinburgh, 1704/1705. [NAS.CH1.2.5.2.149; 175/1]

SANDERS, JOHN, a tailor in Fochabers, Morayshire, and his wife Katherine Simpson, 1705. [NAS.CH1.2.5/187]

SANDISON, ANNA, in the Muir of Glengarden, Aberdeenshire, 1718. [NAS.CH1.2.47.271]

SCOTT, ANDREW, a student at the Scots College at Douai, 1793, later Vicar Apostolic of the Western District. [IR.LVIII.223]

SCOTT, HELEN, an apostate and a 'papist' in Liberton, Edinburgh, 1704. [NAS.CH1.2.5.2.149]

SCOTT, JAMES, a tailor, and his spouse, 'papists' in Canongait, Edinburgh, 1705. [NAS.CH1.2.5.2.170]

SCOTT, JAMES, tenant in Chapelford, parish of Bellie, 1710. [NAS.CH1.2.29.3]

SCOTT, JOHN, a tailor, and his spouse Margaret Scott, 'papists' in Wallace's land below the Earl of Moray's Lodging, Canongait, Edinburgh, 1703/1704. [NAS.CH1.2.5.2/149/151]

SCOTT, MARGARET, wife of John Davidson tenant in Cowie Muir, in the parish of Bellie, 1710. [NAS.CH1.2.29.3/211]

SCOTT, MARGERY, in Fochabers, Morayshire, 1705, wife to James Gordon a tenant in Fochabers, 1710. [NAS.CH1.2.5/2; CH1.2.29.3/210]

SCOTT, MARION, spouse to Robert McPetry, with her children James McPetry, aged eight, and Will, aged six, in Echt, Aberdeenshire, 1704, 1710. [NAS.CH1.2.5.3.194; CH1.2.29.3]

SCOTT, MARJORY, wife to James Gordon a tailor in Fochabers, Morayshire, 1705. [NAS.CH1.2.5/187]

SCOUGALL, JEAN, spouse to Robert Semple the sheriff-depute of Renfrew, in Paisley, Renfrewshire, 1704. [NAS.CH1.2.5.3.202]

SEATON, or ROSS, ALEXANDER, a student at the Scots College at Douai, 1685. [RSC.I.57]

SEATON, ALEXANDER, a glover, and his sister Magdalen Seaton, in Halyburton's land, Monteith's Close, Edinburgh, 'a papist' in College Kirk parish, Edinburgh, 1704/1705. [NAS.CH1.2.5.2.149;175/1]

SEATON, GREGORY, born 1658, died in Ratisbon 1685. [SF#280]

SEATON, ROBERT, a Jesuit priest in Glengarden, Aberdeenshire, 1714, 1718. [NLS.ms976.143] [NAS.CH1.2.47.271]

SEATON, WILLIAM, butler at Traquair, Peebles-shire, 1705. [NAS.CH1.2.5.3/176]

SELLAR, ISOBEL, in the parish of Bellie, 1710. [NAS.CH1.2.29.3/211]

SEMPLE, GEORGE, son of Robert Semple of Glasford and Elizabeth Abercromby, a student at the Scots College in Madrid, 1715. [RSC.I.200]

SEMPLE, HUGH, son of Robert Semple of Glasford and Elizabeth Abercromby, a student at the Scots College in Madrid, 1715. [RSC.I.200]

SEMPLE, JEAN, servant to the laird of Roslyn, in Dalkeith, Midlothian, 1705. [NAS.CH1.2.5/3]

SEMPLE, JEAN, Lady Pitfoddell, 'a papist' in College Kirk parish, Edinburgh, 1704/1705. [NAS.CH1.2.5.2.149;175/1]

SEMPLE, ROBERT, of Dykeside, and his wife Elizabeth Abercrombie, in Greyfriars Kirk parish, Edinburgh, 1704. [NAS.CH1.2.5.154]

SEMPLE, ROBERT, a housekeeper at Gordon Castle, Morayshire, 1705. [NAS.CH1.2.5/187]

SETON, GEORGE, born 1686, son of George Seton of Garleton, a student at the Scots College at Douai, 1698. [RSC.I.64]

SETON, Sir GEORGE, of Garleton, East Lothian, his wife Barbara Wauchop, and children Andrew, Barbara, John, Margaret, and Mary, 1703. [NAS.CH1.2.5.1]

SETON, ANDREW, of Garleton, a student at the Scots College in Madrid, 1715. [RSC.I.200]

SETON, JOHN, born 1668, son of John Seton of Garleton and Christina Hume of Renton, a student at the Scots College at Douai, 1681. [RSC.I.56]

SETON, JOHN, of the Garleton family, a student at the Scots College in Madrid, 1715, died in Edinburgh, 16 July 1757. [RSC.I.199]

SETON, ROBERT, born 1669, son of John Seton of Garleton and Christina Hume of Renton, a student at the Scots College at Douai, 1681. [RSC.I.56]

SHAND, JAMES, a tenant, with his wife Agnes Japs, and son James, in Tullo, Parish of Bellie, 1710. [NAS.CH1.2.29.3/211]

SHAND, JANET, in Fochabers, Morayshire, 1705, 1710. [NAS.CH1.2.5/2; 2.29.3/210]

SHARP, JEAN, in Ruthven, Strathbogie,1710. [NAS.CH1.2.29.3/209]

SHARP, JOHN, a student at the Scots College at Valladolid, 1785, died at Blairs on 5 September 1860. [RSC.I.209]

SHARP, PETER, born 1769 in Mortlach, at Ratisbon Seminary 1784. [SIG#295][RSC.I.254]

SHAW, ADAM, servant to the Setons of Garleton, East Lothian, 1703. [NAS.CH1.2.5.1]

SHAW, ANGUS, and a child, in Ballenicreige, Barra, 1703. [NAS.CH

SHAW, CORNELIUS, and his wife, 'papists' in Liberton, Edinburgh, 1704. [NAS.CH1.2.5.2.149]

SHAW, DONALD, with three children, in Barra, 1703. [NAS.CH1.2.5.1]

SHAW, JANET, spouse to James Grant an officer, in Fochabers, Morayshire, 1705. [NAS.CH1.2.5/187]

SHEARER, JEAN, servant to Lady Graden Ker, 'popish since ten years ago', in South Leith, Edinburgh, 1704. [NAS.CH1.2.5.2.149]

SHEEN, JAMES, a cook at Gordon Castle, Morayshire, 1705. [NAS.CH1.2.5/187]

SHERAR, GEORGE, in Cross, Kinnore parish, 1710. [NAS.CH1.2.29.3/210]

SHORT, ALEXANDER, in Inverarity, Angus, 1704. [NAS.CH1.2.5/204]

SIM, KATHERINE, a maid-servant , a 'papist' in Liberton, Edinburgh, 1704. [NAS.CH1.2.5.2.149]

SIM, MARGARET, in Ruthven, Strathbogie,1710. [NAS.CH1.2.29.3/209]

SIMMISON, CATHERINE, in Cottonhill, Parish of Bellie, 1710. [NAS.CH1.2.29.3/211]

SIMPSON, JEAN, in Ruthven, Strathbogie,1710. [NAS.CH1.2.29.3/209]

SIMSON, GEORGE, a tenant, with his wife Hendriett Innes, and daughter Barbara, in Cottonhill, Parish of Bellie, 1710. [NAS.CH1.2.29.3/211]

SIMSON, JANET, wife of George Simson, in parish of Bellie, 1710. [NAS.CH1.2.29.3]

SINCLAIR, ALEXANDER, of Roslyn, his son William aged four, and his daughter Jean aged seven, in Dalkeith, Midlothian, 1705. [NAS.CH1.2.5/3]

SINCLAIR, GEORGE, a student at the Scots College in Madrid, 1710. [RSC.I.199]

SINCLAIR, JAMES, a student at the Scots College at Valladolid, 1776. [RSC.I.207]

SINCLAIR, THOMAS, brother of the laird of Roslyn, his wife Elisabeth Wauchop, and son James, in Dalkeith, Midlothian, 1705. [NAS.CH1.2.5/3]

SKENE, JAMES, in Fochabers, Morayshire, 1705. [NAS.CH1.2.5/2]

SKINNER, JANET, in Fochabers, Morayshire, 1705. [NAS.CH1.2.5/2]

SKINNER, JOHN, a servant in Fochabers, Morayshire, 1705. [NAS.CH1.2.5/187]

SKINNER, JOHN, a vintner in Keith, Banffshire, 1794. [NAS.SC2.72.4]

SLEGER, MARY, in Conuke, Auchterarder, Perthshire, 1703. [NAS.CH1.2.5.2]

SLOAN, JEAN, spouse to Andrew Wood, in Mabie, Troquair, Orr, Dumfries-shire, 1703, 1705. [NAS.CH1.2.5.1/156]

SLOAN, ROBERT, in Drungans, Traquair, Dumfries-shire, 1703. [NAS.CH1.2.5.1]

SMART, WILLIAM, servant to the laird of Kirkconnel, Dumfries-shire, 1703. [NAS.CH1.2.5.1]

SMART, WILLIAM, a servant to Robert Brown of Bishopton, Dumfries, 1705. [NAS.CH1.2.5.1]

SMITH, ADAM, Parish of Bellie, 1710. [NAS.CH1.2.29.3/211]

SMITH, ALEXANDER, born 1683 in Fochabers, Morayshire, educated at the Scots College in Paris, ordained at Preshome in 1712, Procurator of the Scots College from 1718-1730, Bishop in 1735, died in Edinburgh on 21 August 1767. [SCP#212]

SMITH, ALEXANDER, a smith, with his wife Margaret Lobban, and their children, John, George, Robert, Thomas, and Charles, Parish of Bellie, 1710. [NAS.CH1.2.29.3/211]

SMITH, ANNA, in the parish of Bottarie, Strathbogie, 1710. [NAS.CH1.2.29.3/209]

SMITH, GEORGE, a servant in Nether Achinroth, in the parish of Bellie, 1710. [NAS.CH1.2.29.3/211]

SMITH, GEORGE, under-cook to the Marquess of Huntly, parish of Bellie, 1710. [NAS.CH1.2.29.3]

SMITH, HENRY, and his wife Anna Wilkie, in Whitehill, Inveresk, Edinburgh, 1705. [NAS.CH1.2.5/3]

SMITH, JAMES, a smith in Upper Dallachie, Parish of Bellie, 1710. [NAS.CH1.2.29.3/211]

SMITH, JOHN, at the Raws of Huntly, Dunbennan parish, 1710. [NAS.CH1.2.29.3/210]

SMITH, Dr ROBERT, MD, 'a papist' residing in the house of William Smith a barber in Canongait, Edinburgh, 1703/1704/ 1705. [NAS.CH1.2.5.2.149/151/170]

SMITH, ROBERT, a cottar in Ruthven, Strathbogie,1710. [NAS.CH1.2.29.3/209]

SMITH, THOMAS, a laborer in Banff, Banffshire, 1794. [NAS.SC2.72.4]

SMITH, WILLIAM, a student at the Scots College at Douai, 1793, later at Valladolid. [IR.LVIII.223]

SMYTH, JOHN, his wife Margaret Copland, and daughter Janet Smyth, in Dalbeattie, Orr, Dumfries-shire, 1705. [NAS.CH1.2.5/156]

SMYTH, MARGARET, a servant in Buittle, Kirkcudbrightshire, 1705. [NAS.CH1.2.5.2]

SMYTH, MARY, in Dalbeattie, Orr, Dumfries-shire, 1705. [NAS.CH1.2.5/156]

SMYTH, MARY, spouse of John Speers a cottar in Buittle, Kirkcudbrightshire, 1705. [NAS.CH1.2.5.2]

SOUTAR, DAVID, a servant in Cargill, Perthshire, 1704. [NAS.CH1.2.5.3.203]

SPEER, WILLIAM, a weaver at Castle Semple, Renfrewshire, and his wife Barbara Duncan, 1704.[NAS.CH1.2.5.3.202]

SPENCE, ISOBEL, who stayed with Walter Burne in Con's Close, 1703; lodging in Helen White's house in Stephen Laws Close, Edinburgh, 'a papist' in Tron Kirk parish, Edinburgh, 1704/1705. [NAS.CH1.2.5.2.149/151; 175/1]

SPOTSWOOD, JEAN, mother of the laird of Roslyn, in Dalkeith, Midlothian, 1705. [NAS.CH1.2.5/3]

SPOTSWOOD, JOHN, an advocate in Lasswade, Midlothian, 1704. [NAS.CH1.2.5.2]

STABLE, HELEN, a widow in Nether Achinroth, and her daughters Isobel and Janet Anderson, in the parish of Bellie, 1710. [NAS.CH1.2.29.3/211]

STABLES, JOHN, a servant at Balnacraig, Aboyne or Glentanar, 1710. [NAS.CH1.2.29.3]

STEINSON, MARJORY, wife to John Hutcheon a tenant in Bayrs, Parish of Bellie, 1710. [NAS.CH1.2.29.3/211]

STEINSON, WILLIAM, a tenant in Bray's, with his daughter-in-lawIsobel Mitchell, parish of Bellie, 1710. [NAS.CH1.2.29.3]

STEUART, BARBARA, a 'papist', spouse to William Murray a workman, in College Kirk parish, Edinburgh, 1704. [NAS.CH1.2.5.2/149]

STEVENSON, MARTHA, servant to James Wauchop, 'a papist' in New Kirk parish, Edinburgh, 1704/ 1705. [NAS.CH1.2.5.2.139; 175/1]

STEWART, ALEXANDER, of Clochfoldich, papers, 1678-1689. [SCA.FL1/10]

STEWART, ANTONY, born 1739, a student at Douai, 1751. [RSC.I.88]

STEWART, BEATRIX, in Musselburgh, Midlothian, 1705. [NAS.CH1.2.5/3]

STEWART, BESSIE, born in Castle Gordon, parish of Belly, Banffshire, a spinner in the Musselburgh Woollen Manufactory, 'a papist' in Musselburgh, Edinburgh, 1705. [NAS.CH1.2.5.2.167]

STEWART, CHARLES, 'son to Boggs', 1720. [NLS.ms68.31-32]

STEWART, CHARLES, Earl of Traquair, and his wife Lady Mary Maxwell, Countess of Traquair, Peeblesshire, 1705. [NAS.CH1.2.5.3/176]

STEWART, CHARLES, Lord Linton, later 5th Earl of Traquair, son of Charles Stewart 4th Earl of Traquair and Mary Maxwell, educated at the Scots College in Paris 1715, married Theresa Conyers, died in Edinburgh 24 April 1764. [SCP#214]

STEWART, CHARLES, born 1765, died in Auchendryne on 13 September 1826. [Braemar MI]

STEWART, DUNCAN, a Catholic schoolmaster in Kilmadock, Inverness-shire, 1745. [NAS.CH1.2.85.fos.295-297, 318-319]

STEWART, ISOBEL FORDYCE, in Terregles and Kirkgunzeon, Dumfries-shire, 1705. [NAS.CH1.2.5.2]

STEWART, or TORRIE, JAMES, a student at the Scots College at Valladolid, 1777. [RSC.I.207]

STEWART, JANET, servant to William Badenoch, formerly in Kinnore, now in Rothiemay, Strathbogie, 1710. [NAS.CH1.2.29.3]

STEWART, JOHN, of Clochfoldich, papers, 1690-1698. [SCA.FL1/11]

STEWART, JOHN, son of Alexander Stewart, a merchant in Old Aberdeen, and Isobel Collie, Protestants, who was baptised as a Protestant when an infant, was baptised by on 29 September 1697 by Father Robert Francis. [SNQ.VIII.182]

STEWART, JOHN, a weaver's servant in Aberdeen, 1704/1705. [NAS.CH1.2.5.2/155]

STEWART, JOHN, a Jacobite captured at the Siege of Preston, transported from Liverpool aboard the Scipio bound for Antigua, 30 March 1716, there from 1716 to 1718. [SPAWI.1716.310][CTB.XXXI.204][SCA.FL1/18]

STEWART, JOHN, in Milton, with his wife and son John Stewart, in Glengarden, Aberdeenshire, 1718. [NAS.CH1.2.47.271]

STEWART, JOHN, of Balatuach the elder, in Glenmuick, Aberdeenshire, and his son John Stewart, 1714, 1718. [NLS.ms976.143] [NAS.CH1.2.47.271]

STEWART, WILLIAM, of Achoily, Alexander Stewart of Achoily the younger, and William's children Isobel, Jean, Helen, and James, in Glengarden, Aberdeenshire, 1718. [NAS.CH1.2.47.271]

STEWART, Lady, in Smith's Newland, College Kirk parish, Edinburgh, 1703. [NAS.CH1.2.5.2/151]

STILL, JEAN, and her daughter at the Raws of Huntly, Dunbennan parish, 1710. [NAS.CH1.2.29.3/210]

STILL, JOHN, in Ruthven, Strathbogie,1710. [NAS.CH1.2.29.3/209]

STIRGEON, JANET, in Terregles and Kirkgunzeon, Dumfries-shire, 1705. [NAS.CH1.2.5.2]

STITCHELL, GEORGE, at the Raws of Huntly, Dunbennan parish, 1710.
[NAS.CH1.2.29.3/210]

STITCHELL, GEORGE, in Robestoun, Kinnoir parish, 1710. [NAS.CH1.2.29.3/210]

STITCHELL, JAMES, at the Raws of Huntly, Dunbennan parish, 1710.
[NAS.CH1.2.29.3/210]

STITCHELL, JEAN, at the Raws of Huntly, Dunbennan parish, 1710.
[NAS.CH1.2.29.3/210]

STITCHELL, PETER, at the Raws of Huntly, Dunbennan parish, 1710.
[NAS.CH1.2.29.3/210]

STITCHELL, THOMAS, and his wife Isobel Robson, at the Raws of Huntly,
Dunbennan parish, 1710. [NAS.CH1.2.29.3/210]

STITCHELL, WILLIAM, at the Raws of Huntly, Dunbennan parish, 1710.
[NAS.CH1.2.29.3/210]

STRACHAN, ALEXANDER, and his spouse Margaret Thomson, in Edinburgh,
apostates and 'papists' in Newbyth's land, Tron Kirk parish, Edinburgh,
1703/1704/1705. He keeps a school for sewing, playing and singing, and has
two of the Earl of Traquair's daughters lodging in his house.
[NAS.CH1.2.5.2.149/151;175/1]

STRACHAN, ANNA, in Fettercairn, Kincardineshire, daughter of James Strachan
of Thornton, Aberlethnot, Kincardineshire, 1704. [NAS.CH1.2.5.3/201]

STRACHAN, BARBARA, servant to the Earl of Nithsdale, in Terregles, Dumfries-
shire, 1703. [NAS.CH1.2.5.1]

STRACHAN, or RAMSAY, HUGH, born 1672, son of James Strachan of Thornton
and Catherine Ross of Pittendrich, a student at the Scots College at Douai,
1693; a priest in Ardoch, Glengarden, Aberdeenshire, 1714, 1718.
[RSC.I.62][NLS.ms976.143][NAS.CH1.2.47.271; CH1.2.29.3/208]

STRACHAN, KENNETH FRANCIS, baron of Thornton, a student at the Scots
College at Douai, 1700; rector of the Scots College at Madrid, 1725.
[RSC.I.65/203]

STRACHAN, PETER, a clerk in Earnhill, in Ruthven, Strathbogie,1710. [NAS.CH1.2.29.3/209]

STRACHAN, ROBERT, born 15 September 1737, son of Alexander Strachan and Joanna Bremner, a student at Douai, 1758. [RSC.I.91]

STRATTEN, Mrs, in Terregles, Dumfries-shire, 1703. [NAS.CH1.2.5.1]

STRONACH, ELSPET, a tenant woman in Parish of Bellie, 1710. [NAS.CH1.2.29.3/211]

STRONACH, GEORGE, and his spouse Beatrix Ross, in Fochabers, Morayshire, 1705. [NAS.CH1.2.5/187]

STRONACH, GEORGE, chamberlain to the Duke, and Janet Stewart his wife, in Fochabers, 1710. [NAS.CH1.2.29.3/210]

STRONACH, GEORGE, tenant, with his wife Marjory Sinclair, Parish of Bellie, 1710. [NAS.CH1.2.29.3/211]

STRONACH, ISOBEL, and her children Margaret, Bettie, Barbara, and William, in Boghead, parish of Bellie, 1710. [NAS.CH1.2.29.3]

STRONACH, MARGARET, a spinner in the Musselburgh Woollen Manufactory, 'a papist' in Musselburgh, Edinburgh, 1705. [NAS.CH1.2.5.2/167; 3/182]

STUART, ALEXANDER, and his wife Helen Gordon, Strathaven, Banffshire, 1708. [NAS.CH1.2.30/1/28]

STUART, ALEXANDER, at Ratisbon Seminary 1718. [SIG#294][RSC.I.250]

STUART, Lady BARBARA, of Traquair, accounts, 1736-1743. [SCA.FL4/1]

STUART, BETTY, a convert, daughter of Sir John Stuart of Allanbank, married Don Antonio Cicciaporci an officer in the Pope's guards, on 21 January 1782 in London. [IR.XVII.46]

STUART, CHARLES, and his wife Katharine Grant, in Cults, Strathaven, Banffshire, 1708. [NAS.CH1.2.30/1/28]

STUART, CHARLES, born 1709, at Ratisbon Seminary 1719. [SIG#294][RSC.I.251]

STUART, CHARLES, born 1753, son of Robert Stuart and Claudia Gairden, a student at Douai, 1766. [RSC.I.93]

STUART, DONALD, in Achrahan, and his wife Janet Forbes, in Strathaven, Banffshire, 1708. [NAS.CH1.2.30/1/28]

STUART, JAMES, in Acherahan, Strathaven, Banffshire, 1708. [NAS.CH1.2.30/1/28]

STUART, JAMES, miller at Delnabo, and his wife Marjorie Gregorach, in Strathaven, Banffshire, 1708. [NAS.CH1.2.30/1/28]

STUART, JAMES, at Ratisbon Seminary 1718. [SIG#294][RSC.I.250]

STUART, JAMES, born 1734, at Ratisbon Seminary 1747. [SIG#294][RSC.I.252]

STUART, JOHN, in Achrahan, withe his wife Mary Grant, Strathaven, Banffshire, 1708. [NAS.CH1.2.30/1/28]

STUART, or MCALLAN, JOHN, and his wife Elspet Ross, Strathaven, Banffshire, 1708. [NAS.CH1.2.30/1/28]

STUART, JOHN, of Bogs, born 29 June 1702, died 7 July 1780. [Bellie Tynet gravestone]

STUART, JOHN, at Ratisbon Seminary 1713. [SIG#294][RSC.I.250]

STUART, JOHN, born 1731, at Ratisbon Seminary 1747. [SIG#294][RSC.I.252]

STUART, JOHN, son of Robert Stuart and Claudia Gairden, a student at Douai, 1766. [RSC.I.93]

STUART, MAURICE, of Aina, Diocese of Aberdeen, at Ratisbon Seminary 1692, a Professor in Prague by 1697, died 1720. [SIG#293]

STUART, PATRICK, at Ratisbon Seminary 1719. [SIG#294][RSC.I.251]

STUART, WILLIAM, and his wife Beatrix Riach, with children Margaret, William, Mary, and Anna, in Torviebeg, Botriphnie, 1710. [NAS.CH1.2.29.3/209]

STURGEON, ANNA, in Munches, in Buittle, Kirkcudbrightshire, 1705. [NAS.CH1.2.5.2]

STURGEON, JOHN, tenant in Kirkbean, Orr, Dumfries-shire, 1705. [NAS.CH1.2.5/156]

STURGEON, MARGARET, servant to Thomas Maxwell in Aird of Kirkconnel, New Abbey, Dumfries-shire, 1703. [NAS.CH1.2.5.1]

SUTHERLAND, ANGUS, a butcher in Fochabers, his wife Agnes McConachie, and children Anna and George, Morayshire, 1705, 1710. [NAS.CH1.2.5/2; 2.29.3/210]

SUTHERLAND, ANNE, servant to the Marquess of Sutherland, parish of Bellie, 1710. [NAS.CH1.2.29.3]

SUTHERLAND, GEORGE, a weaver's servant in Fochabers, 1710. [NAS.CH1.2.29.3/210]

SUTHERLAND, ISOBEL, a servant in Cowie Muir, in the parish of Bellie, 1710. [NAS.CH1.2.29.3/211]

SWAN, MARION, a servant to the Duchess of Gordon, 'a papist' in Canongait, Edinburgh, 1705. [NAS.CH1.2.5.2.170]

SYMER, MARGARET, in Tullo, Parish of Bellie, 1710. [NAS.CH1.2.29.3/211]

SYMON, ANNE, servant in Tullo, Parish of Bellie, 1710. [NAS.CH1.2.29.3/211]

SYMON, JOHN, a tailor in Ardach, with his wife Anne Forbes, in Glenmuick, Tullich, and Glengarden, Aberdeenshire, 1718. [NAS.CH1.2.47/284]

SYMON, PETER, the younger, servant in Bray's, parish of Bellie, 1710. [NAS.CH1.2.29.3]

SYMON, WILLIAM, a sub-tenant, and his daughter Anne, in Tullo, Parish of Bellie, 1710. [NAS.CH1.2.29.3/211]

TAINS, ISOBEL, wife of Thomas More at Drummond, Auchterarder, Perthshire, 1703. [NAS.CH1.2.5.2]

TAYLOR, ALEXANDER, a tailor, with his mother Bessie Gordon, in Tullo, Parish of Bellie, 1710. [NAS.CH1.2.29.3/211]

TAYLOR, ELSPET, in Ruthven, Strathbogie,1710. [NAS.CH1.2.29.3/209]

TAYLOR, ELSPET, in Culorne, Kinnoir parish, 1710. [NAS.CH1.2.29.3/210]

TAYLOR, ISOBEL, wife to Alexander Williamson in Nether Dallachie, in the parish of Bellie, 1710. [NAS.CH1.2.29.3/211]

TAYLOR, JANET, wife to Alexander Morrison, in Nether Dallachie, in the parish of Bellie, 1710. [NAS.CH1.2.29.3/211]

TAYLOR, MARGARET, a widow in Beldornie, Glass, 1710. [NAS.CH1.2.29.3]

TAYLOR, MARGARET, Parish of Bellie, 1710. [NAS.CH1.2.29.3/211]

TAYLOR, MARGARET, a tenant in Upper Dallachie, with her daughter Isobel Gray, Parish of Bellie, 1710. [NAS.CH1.2.29.3/211]

TAYLOR, MARY, in Brunston, Kinnoir parish, 1710. [NAS.CH1.2.29.3/210]

TAYLOR, PETER, tenant in Upper Dallachie, in the parish of Bellie, 1710. [NAS.CH1.2.29.3/211]

THOMSON, AGNES, in Richorne, Orr, Dumfries-shire, 1705. [NAS.CH1.2.5/156]

THOMSON, BARBARA, a servant in Buittle, Kirkcudbrightshire, 1705. [NAS.CH1.2.5.2]

THOMSON, DANIEL, in Peebles Wynd, Edinburgh, 'a papist' in Tron Kirk parish, Edinburgh, 1705. [NAS.CH1.2.5.2.175/1]

THOMSON, ISOBEL, in Earnhill, Ruthven, Strathbogie,1710. [NAS.CH1.2.29.3/209]

THOMSON, JAMES, son of Thomas Thomson and Louisa Shand in Aberdeen, a student at the Scots College in Madrid, 1734. [RSC.I.200]

THOMSON, JANET, in Dumfries, 1704. [NAS.CH1.5.2]

THOMSON, JANET, spouse to John Walker, in Richorne, Orr, Dumfries-shire, 1705. [NAS.CH1.2.5/156]

THOMSON, JANET, a servant in Buittle, Kirkcudbrightshire, 1705. [NAS.CH1.2.5.2]

THOMSON, JEAN, in Colvend, Dumfries-shire, 1704. [NAS.CH1.2.5.2]

THOMSON, JEAN, in Rigside, Dumfries-shire, 1704. [NAS.CH1.5.2]

THOMSON, JOHN, in Richorne, Orr, Dumfries-shire, 1705. [NAS.CH1.2.5/156]

THOMSON, JOHN, a servant in Buittle, Kirkcudbrightshire, 1705. [NAS.CH1.2.5.2]

THOMSON, JOHN, tenant in Bray's, with his wife Marjory Cuie, and sons James and John, parish of Bellie, 1710. [NAS.CH1.2.29.3]

THOMSON, MARGARET, a schoolmistress in Tron Kirk parish, Edinburgh, 1703, spouse of Alexander Strachan in Kinloch's Close, Edinburgh. [NAS.CH1.2.5.2/151/153]

THOMSON, MARION, a widow in Dumfries, 1705. [NAS.CH1.2.5.1]

THOMSON, MARION, in Rigside, Dumfries, 1704. [NAS.CH1.5.2]

THOMSON, SQUIRE, in Inveresk, Midlothian, in the house of Robert Gibb, 1705. [NAS.CH1.2.5/3]

THOMSON, WILLIAM, son to the late Sir William Thomson town clerk of Edinburgh, an apostate, a 'papist' in Campbell's land, the Canongait, Edinburgh, 1703/ 1704. [NAS.CH1.2.5.2/149/151]

THOMSON, WILLIAM, a gentleman in Carnbie, 'a papist' in Fife, 1705. [NAS.CH1.2.5.2.174/2]

TINNING, MARION, tenant or cottar in Cargan, Traquair, Dumfries-shire, 1703. [NAS.CH1.2.5.1]

TROTTER, JOHN, and his spouse Christian Dunbar, in Clark's Land, Edinburgh, ' papists' in College Kirk parish, Edinburgh, 1704/1705. [NAS.CH1.2.5.2.149/171]

TULLOCH, AGNES, in Ruthven, Strathbogie,1710. [NAS.CH1.2.29.3/209]

TYRIE, ADAM, a student at the Scots College in Valladolid, 1770, died 25 April 1775. [RSC.I.205]

TYRIE, JOHN, born 1695 in Insch, ordained in Rome during 1719, priest in Strathbogie, Scalan, Morar, and Glenlivet, a Jacobite at Culloden, took refuge in Glenlivet, died at Shenval in the Cabrach in 1755. [IR.XVIII.136]

URQUHART, ADAM, brother of the Baron of Meldrum, a student at the Scots College at Douai, 16891. [RSC.I.60]

URQUHART, CHARLES, born 1 August 1668, son of Thomas Urquhart and Anna Adamson, a student at the Scots College at Douai, 1681. [RSC.I.55]

URQUHART, ELIZABETH, spouse to Andrew Burnet in Tillifoudie, Aboyne or Glentanar, Aberdeenshire, 1704, 1710. [NAS.CH1.2.5/190; CH1.2.29.3]

URQUHART, LUDOVICK, born 1680, a student at the Scots College at Douai, 1695. [RSC.I.63]

VAN DER BERGH, JACOBA, spouse then relict of Sergeant Michael Sinclair of the Foot Guards, 'a papist' in Canongait, Edinburgh, 1703/1704/1705. [NAS.CH1.2.5.2.149/151/170]

VAN DER SYPIUS, JOHN, a limner, and his spouse Margaret Sturgeon, 'papists' in Canongait, Edinburgh, 1703/1705. [NAS.CH1.2.5.2.151/170]

VAN SIPPO, JAN, a japanner, and his spouse Margaret Strogan, 'papists' in College Kirk parish, Edinburgh, 1704/1705. [NAS.CH1.2.5.2.149;175/1]

VEITCH, JAMES, a card-maker and a 'papist' in Glen'our's land, College Kirk parish, Edinburgh, 1704. [NAS.CH1.2.5.2/149]

VILONG, LOUIS, 'came from France upwards of twenty years ago', a prawn gatherer in Leith, 'a papist' in South Leith, later in Canongait, Edinburgh, 1704,1705. [NAS.CH1.2.5.2.149/170]

VEILLAN, JOHN JOSEPH, from the diocese of St Andrews, educated at the Scots College in Paris before 1716, died in Edinburgh on 18 October 1719. [SCP#214]

WACHOP, JEAN, widow of Robert Menzies in the Mill of Gilcomston, was baptised in Aberdeen by Father Robert Francis on 18 January 1698. [SNQ.VIII.182]

WALKER, AGNES, spouse to Alexander Marshall an indweller in Edinburgh, 'a papist' in Con's Close, Tron Kirk parish, Edinburgh, 1703/1704/1705. [NAS.CH1.2.5.2.149/151; 175/1]

WALKER, EUPHAN, servant to Robert Brownhill in Athelstoneford, East Lothian, 1703. [NAS.CH1.2.5.1]

WALKER, JAMES, servant to Andrew Chisholm, a tenant in Muirhouse, East Lothian, 1703. [NAS.CH1.2.5.1]

WALKER, WILLIAM, hind in the Mains of Garleton, East Lothian, with five children, 1703. [NAS.CH1.2.5.1]

WALLACE, JOHN, born in Arbroath 1654, son of Provost Patrick Wallace, a former Episcopalian preacher, at the Scots College in Paris 1687, in Arbroath, Angus, 1704, ordained at Preshome in 1708, Bishop of Edinburgh 1720, died in Edinburgh on 30 June 1733. [NAS.CH1.2.5.3.186][SCP#211]

WALLACE, WILLIAM, a wright in Stonehaven, Kincardineshire, 1705. [NAS.CH1.2.5.2]

WALLACE, WILLIAM, a student at the Scots College at Douai, 1793, later a commissioner at Traquair. [IR.LVIII.223]

WATSON, PAUL, and his wife Jean Still, in Easter Cambdel, Strathaven, Banffshire, 1708. [NAS.CH1.2.30/1/28]

WATT, JOHN, a weaver in Nether Dallachie, with his wife Janet Paterson, in the parish of Bellie, 1710. [NAS.CH1.2.29.3/211]

WATTIE, JOHN, in Foran, Glengarden, Aberdeenshire, 1718. [NAS.CH1.2.47.271]

WAUCHOP, JAMES, son of Andrew Wauchop of Nithry, a student at the Scots College at Douai, 1692. [RSC.I.61]

WAUCHOP, WILLIAM, son of Andrew Wauchop of Nithry, a student at the Scots College at Douai, 1692. [RSC.I.61]

WAUCHOP, ..., laird of Niddry, his wife, and children Andrew, Jean, and James, in Liberton, Edinburgh, 1704. [NAS.CH1.2.5.154]

WAUCHOP, ELIZABETH, spouse to James Sinclair, and their son, in Lasswade, Midlothian, 1704. [NAS.CH1.2.5.2]

WAUCHOP, GILBERT, born 1684, son of Andrew Wauchop of Niddrie-Marischal, educated at the Scots College in Paris, later a doctor of medicine, died 15 May 1747. [SCP#212]

WAUCHOP, JAMES, merchant in Edinburgh, son of the Laird of Niddry,' a papist' in Mary King's Close, New Kirk parish and later Liberton, Edinburgh, 1704/1705. [NAS.CH1.2.5.2.149/154; 175/1]

WAUCHOP, WILLIAM, second son of the laird of Niddrie, a 'papist' in Liberton, Edinburgh, 1704. [NAS.CH1.2.5.2.149]

WAUCHOP, ..., laird of Niddrie, 'a papist' in Liberton, Edinburgh, 1681. [RPCS.VII.728]

WEBSTER, BESSIE, and her sister Jean Webster, in Brunston, Kinnoir parish, 1710. [NAS.CH1.2.29.3/210]

WEIR, MARGARET, wife of James Badenoch, and sons James, John, and George, 'baptised by the priest', parish of Bellie, 1710. [NAS.CH1.2.29.3]

WELCH, JAMES, a card maker in Edinburgh, 'a papist' in College Kirk parish, Edinburgh, 1703/1705. [NAS.CH1.2.5.2.151/175/1]

WHITE, FRANCIS, an Irish priest in Lochaber and Glengarry during 1660s and 1670s. [IR.XXIV.80]

WHITE, JEAN, a widow in Echt, Aberdeenshire, with her children James Hay and Henrietta Hay, 1704. [NAS.CH1.2.5.3.194]

WHYTE, ANNA, relict of William Schoterum, in Liberton's Wynd, Edinburgh, 'a papist' in New North Kirk parish, later in Tron Kirk parish, Edinburgh, 1704/1705. [NAS.CH1.2.5.2.149/154; 175/1]

WHYTEFORD, Colonel, of HM Guards, removed from duty, 1674. [RPCS.IV.124]

WILLIAMSON, DAVID, in Colvend, Dumfries-shire, 1704. [NAS.CH1.2.5.2]

WILLIAMSON, JANET, a servant at Milne of Kinnoir, Kinnoir parish, 1710. [NAS.CH1.2.29.3/210]

WILLIAMSON, JOHN, in Colvend, Dumfries-shire, 1704. [NAS.CH1.2.5.2]

WILLIAMSON, THOMAS, in Colvend, Dumfries-shire, 1704. [NAS.CH1.2.5.2]

WILLIAMSON, THOMAS, and his wife Katharine Martin, Strathaven, Banffshire, 1708. [NAS.CH1.2.30/1/28]

WILSON, ANDREW, in Ruthven, Strathbogie,1710. [NAS.CH1.2.29.3/209]

WILSON, BARBARA, a servant in Kirkbean, Orr, Dumfries-shire, 1705. [NAS.CH1.2.5/156]

WILSON, EDWARD, of Burntslick (?)in Buittle, Kirkcudbrightshire, 1705. [NAS.CH1.2.5.2]

WILSON, GEORGE, a cottar in Orchardton, with his wife Barbara Wyllie, in Buittle, Kirkcudbrightshire, 1705. [NAS.CH1.2.5.2]

WILSON, JAMES, a cottar in Munches, with Mary Lindsay his wife, and children – James, Barbara, Margaret, and Agnes, in Buittle, Kirkcudbrightshire, 1705. [NAS.CH1.2.5.2]

WILSON or MCCULLOCH, JAMES, born 15 May 1750, son of William McCulloch (a non Catholic) and Joanna Runcie (a Catholic), a student at Douai 1763. [RSC.I.92]

WILSON, JANET, in the parish of Bottarie, Strathbogie, 1710. [NAS.CH1.2.29.3/209]

WILSON, JEAN, in Gray's Close, spouse to James Frazer a soldier in Edinburgh Castle, an apostate and 'a papist' in College Kirk parish, Edinburgh, 1703,1704, 1705. [NAS.CH1.2.5.2.149/151/175/1]

WILSON, JOHN, in Dalbeattie, Orr, Dumfries-shire, 1705. [NAS.CH1.2.5/156]

WILSON, JOHN, with his sister Jean, and his aunt Janet Wilson, in Dalbeattie, Orr, Dumfries-shire, 1705. [NAS.CH1.2.5/156]

WILSON, JOHN, a weaver, with his sister Margaret Wilson, parish of Bellie, 1710. [NAS.CH1.2.29.3]

WILSON, MARGARET, in Dalbeattie, Orr, Dumfries-shire, 1705. [NAS.CH1.2.5/156]

WILSON, NICOLAS, in Dalbeattie, Orr, Dumfries-shire, 1705. [NAS.CH1.2.5/156]

WILSON, SYBELLA, servant to John Chancellor, 'a papist' in College Kirk parish, Edinburgh, 1704/1705. [NAS.CH1.2.5.2.149;175/1]

WINCHESTER, ALEXANDER, born around 1625 in Garmouth, Morayshire, ordained in Rome 1656, Prefect Apostolic of Scotland from 1662 to 1697, died in Banff, 14 January 1708. [[CDS]

WINSTER, MARY, daughter of the late Peter Winster a vintner, in Canongait, Edinburgh, 1703. [NAS.CH1.2.5.2]

WINTON, BESSIE, in Ruthven, Strathbogie,1710. [NAS.CH1.2.29.3/209]

WISHART, HENRY, in Fochabers, Morayshire, 1705; a gardener, with his son Robert,in Fochabers, 1710. [NAS.CH1.2.5/2; 2.29.3/210]

WISHART, JAMES, a park-keeper in Fochabers, and his wife Marjory Achamachie, 1710. [NAS.CH1.2.29.3/210]

WISHART, JEAN, in Fochabers, Morayshire, 1705. [NAS.CH1.2.5/2]

WISHART, or DONALDSON, JOHN, born 1633, son of William Wishart and Joanna Cunningham, a student at the Scots College at Douai, 1681. [RSC.I.55]

WISHART, ROBERT, in Fochabers, Morayshire, 1705. [NAS.CH1.2.5/2]

WOLFE, JAMES, a servant in College Kirk parish, Edinburgh, 1705.[NAS.CH1.2.5.2]

WOOD, ANDREW, the younger, late laird of Balbegno, now in New Thornton, Aberlethnot, Kincardineshire, 1704. [NAS.CH1.2.5.3/201]

WOOD, GEORGE, a student at the Scots College at Douai, 1690, and at the Scots College in Madrid, 1693. [RSC.I.60/199]

WOOD, JAMES, in Milnhill of Kirkconnel, Dumfries-shire, 1703. [NAS.CH1.2.5.1]

WOOD, Captain JOHN, and his wife Margaret Hamilton, a schoolmistress, and their son, in Cant's Close, Edinburgh, 'papists' in Cant's Close, Tron Kirk parish, Edinburgh, 1703/1704/ 1705. At present abroad. [NAS.CH1.2.5.2.149/151/175/1]

WRIGHT, ELIZABETH, in Troquair, Orr, Dumfries-shire, 1705.
[NAS.CH1.2.5/156]

WRIGHT, HEW, in Terregles and Kirkgunzeon, Dumfries-shire, 1705.
[NAS.CH1.2.5.2]

WRIGHT, ISOBEL, servant in Cargan, Traquair, Dumfries-shire, 1703.
[NAS.CH1.2.5.1]

WRIGHT, ISOBEL, spouse to John Walls, in Troquair, Orr, Dumfries-shire, 1705.
[NAS.CH1.2.5/156]

WRIGHT, JANET, in Greenmerse, New Abbey, Dumfries-shire, 1703.
[NAS.CH1.2.5.1]

WRIGHT, JANET, in Terregles and Kirkgunzeon, Dumfries-shire, 1705.
[NAS.CH1.2.5.2]

WRIGHT, JOHN, servant to George Maxwell in Carruchen, Traquair, Dumfries-shire, 1703. [NAS.CH1.2.5.1]

WRIGHT, JOHN, in Troquair, Orr, Dumfries-shire, 1705. [NAS.CH1.2.5/156]

WRIGHT, JOHN, his wife Barbara Carlyle, and children Agnes, Elizabeth, Isobel, Margaret, Mary, in Troquair, Orr, Dumfries-shire, 1703, 1705.
[NAS.CH1.2.5.1/156]

WRIGHT, MARGARET, servant to the laird of Kirkconnel, New Abbey, Dumfries-shire, 1703. [NAS.CH1.2.5.1]

WRIGHT, MARGARET, tenant or cottar in Cargan, Traquair, Dumfries-shire, 1703. [NAS.CH1.2.5.1]

WRIGHT, MARGARET, in Dalbeattie, Orr, Dumfries-shire, 1705.
[NAS.CH1.2.5/156]

WRIGHT, MARGARET, Orr, Dumfries-shire, 1705. [NAS.CH1.2.5/156]

WRIGHT, ROBERT, and spouse Janet Wright, in Troquair, Orr, Dumfries-shire, 1703, 1705. [NAS.CH1.2.5.1/156]

WRIGHT, ROBERT, his spouse Marion Rigg, in Troquair, Orr, Dumfries-shire, 1705. [NAS.CH1.2.5/156]

WRIGHT, WILLIAM, and his daughter Janet, in Cargan, Troquair, Orr, Dumfries-shire, 1705. [NAS.CH1.2.5.1/156]

WYLANS, ISOBEL, parish of Bellie, 1710. [NAS.CH1.2.29.3]

WYLANS, JAMES, tenant in Tynett, with his wife Margaret L'Ommie, in the parish of Bellie, 1710. [NAS.CH1.2.29.3/211]

YEAMAN, JEAN, spouse of Thomas Pagan in Borgue, Kirkcudbrightshire, 1705. [NAS.CH1.2.5.2]

YOUNG, ALEXANDER, at Ratisbon Seminary, 1772. [SIG#295][RSC.I.253]

YOUNG, ARTHUR, in Achairn, with his wife Grizell Anderson also sons William and Nathaniel, daughters Jean, Katherine, and Helen, in the parish of Bottarie, Strathbogie, 1710. [NAS.CH1.2.29.3/209]

YOUNG, GEORGE, a priest imprisoned in Edinburgh Tolbooth, transferred to the Bass Rock, 1679. [RPCS.VI.100]

YOUNG, JANET, in Fochabers, Morayshire, 1705. [NAS.CH1.2.5/2]

YOUNG, JANET, and her son George Robertson, in Cottonhill, Parish of Bellie, 1710. [NAS.CH1.2.29.3/211]

YOUNG, ..., relict of Robert Dunbar, in Stephen Laws Close, Edinburgh, 'a papist' in Old Kirk parish, Edinburgh, 1704/1705. [NAS.CH1.2.5.2.149/175/1]

SOME SCOTTISH CATHOLIC EMIGRANTS TO NORTH AMERICA

Passengers aboard the Alexander

CAMERON, DONALD, from Acharacle, Ardnamurchan, emigrated aboard the brig Alexander of Greenock in June 1772, landed at Charlottetown, Prince Edward Island, on 25 June 1772. [PAPEI#2664/140,140]

CAMERON, DOUGALD, from Acharacle, Ardnamurchan, emigrated aboard the brig Alexander of Greenock in June 1772, landed at Charlottetown, Prince Edward Island, on 25 June 1772. [PAPEI#2664/140,152]

CUMMING, JOHN, from Boisdale, South Uist, emigrated aboard the brig Alexander of Greenock in June 1772, landed at Charlottetown, Prince Edward Island, on 25 June 1772. [PAPEI#2664/151]

GILLIES, DONALD, from Brunacory, North Morar, emigrated aboard the brig Alexander of Greenock in June 1772, landed at Charlottetown, Prince Edward Island, on 25 June 1772. [PAPEI#2664/138]

HENDERSON, DONALD, and his wife, from Eigg, emigrated aboard the brig Alexander of Greenock in June 1772, landed at Charlottetown, Prince Edward Island, on 25 June 1772. [PAPEI#2664/142]

HENDERSON, NEIL, from Eigg, emigrated aboard the brig Alexander of Greenock in June 1772, landed at Charlottetown, Prince Edward Island, on 25 June 1772. [PAPEI#2664/142]

MCCORMIG, ANGUS, from Boisdale, South Uist, emigrated aboard the brig Alexander of Greenock in June 1772, landed at Charlottetown, Prince Edward Island, on 25 June 1772. [PAPEI#2664/151]

MACDONALD, ALEXANDER, from Morar, emigrated aboard the brig Alexander of Greenock in June 1772, landed at Charlottetown, Prince Edward Island, on 25 June 1772. [PAPEI#2664/71,144,147]

MAC DONALD, ALEXANDER, from Eigg, emigrated aboard the brig <u>Alexander of Greenock</u> in June 1772, landed at Charlottetown, Prince Edward Island, on 25 June 1772. [PAPEI#2664/142]

MAC DONALD, ALEXANDER, from Cornua, emigrated aboard the brig <u>Alexander of Greenock</u> in June 1772, landed at Charlottetown, Prince Edward Island, on 25 June 1772. [PAPEI#2664/139, 149]

MAC DONALD, ANGUS, from Boisdale, South Uist emigrated aboard the brig <u>Alexander of Greenock</u> in June 1772, landed at Charlottetown, Prince Edward Island, on 25 June 1772. [PAPEI#2664/151]

MACDONALD, ANGUS, from Corinua,t emigrated aboard the brig <u>Alexander of Greenock</u> in June 1772, landed at Charlottetown, Prince Edward Island, on 25 June 1772. [PAPEI#2664/149, 139]

MAC DONALD, DONALD, from Bornish, South Uist emigrated aboard the brig <u>Alexander of Greenock</u> in June 1772, landed at Charlottetown, Prince Edward Island, on 25 June 1772. [PAPEI#2664/138]

MAC DONALD, DONALD, from Borrodale, emigrated aboard the brig <u>Alexander of Greenock</u> in June 1772, landed at Charlottetown, Prince Edward Island, on 25 June 1772. [PAPEI#2664/153]

MAC DONALD, JAMES, born 1736, a Catholic priest from Moidart, emigrated aboard the brig <u>Alexander of Greenock</u> in June 1772, landed at Charlottetown, Prince Edward Island, on 25 June 1772. [SCA.BL3.242/2; BL3.288/9,10]

MAC DONALD, JOHN, from Stonybridge, Boisdale, South Uist emigrated aboard the brig <u>Alexander of Greenock</u> in June 1772, landed at Charlottetown, Prince Edward Island, on 25 June 1772. [PAPEI#2664/151]

MAC DONALD, RANALD, from Boisdale, South Uist emigrated aboard the brig <u>Alexander of Greenock</u> in June 1772, landed at Charlottetown, Prince Edward Island, on 25 June 1772. [PAPEI#2664/151]

MAC DONALD, RANALD, from Alassay emigrated aboard the brig <u>Alexander of Greenock</u> in June 1772, landed at Charlottetown, Prince Edward Island, on 25 June 1772. [PAPEI#2664/139, 141, 149.]

MACDONALD, RORY or RODERICK, a physician from Eigg. [PAPEI]

MACEACHERN, DONALD, son of Ewan MacEachern, from Kinlochmoidart, emigrated aboard the brig <u>Alexander of Greenock</u> in June 1772, landed at Charlottetown, Prince Edward Island, on 25 June 1772. [PAPEI#2664/71, 144, 147]

MACEACHERN, EWAN, from Kinlochmoidart, emigrated aboard the brig <u>Alexander of Greenock</u> in June 1772, landed at Charlottetown, Prince Edward Island, on 25 June 1772. [PAPEI#2664/70, 150]

MACEACHERN, HUGH BAN, from Kinlochmoidart, emigrated aboard the brig <u>Alexander of Greenock</u> in June 1772, landed at Charlottetown, Prince Edward Island, on 25 June 1772. [PAPEI#2664/153]

MACFIE, DONALD, emigrated aboard the brig <u>Alexander of Greenock</u> in June 1772, landed at Charlottetown, Prince Edward Island, on 25 June 1772. [PAPEI#2664/7][SCA.BL3/247/7]

MCGRAW, ALEXANDER, from Moidart, emigrated aboard the brig <u>Alexander of Greenock</u> in June 1772, landed at Charlottetown, Prince Edward Island, on 25 June 1772. [SCA.BL3.242/2]

MCINNIS, DONALD, from Barra, emigrated aboard the brig <u>Alexander of Greenock</u> in June 1772, landed at Charlottetown, Prince Edward Island, on 25 June 1772. [PAPEI#2664/151]

MCINNIS, DUNCAN, from Boisdale, South Uist, emigrated aboard the brig <u>Alexander of Greenock</u> in June 1772, landed at Charlottetown, Prince Edward Island, on 25 June 1772. [PAPEI#2664/151]

MCINNIS, ..., a mason, emigrated aboard the brig <u>Alexander of Greenock</u> in June 1772, landed at Charlottetown, Prince Edward Island, on 25 June 1772. [SCA.BL3.248/1]

MCINTOSH, DONALD, from Boisdale, South Uist, emigrated aboard the brig <u>Alexander of Greenock</u> in June 1772, landed at Charlottetown, Prince Edward Island, on 25 June 1772. [PAPEI#2664/151]

MCINTYRE, ANGUS, from Barra, emigrated aboard the brig <u>Alexander of Greenock</u> in June 1772, landed at Charlottetown, Prince Edward Island, on 25 June 1772. [PAPEI#2664/151]

MCINTYRE, JOHN, from Boisdale, South Uist, emigrated aboard the brig <u>Alexander of Greenock</u> in June 1772, landed at Charlottetown, Prince Edward Island, on 25 June 1772. [PAPEI#2664/151]

MCINTYRE, JOHN, from Barra, emigrated aboard the brig <u>Alexander of Greenock</u> in June 1772, landed at Charlottetown, Prince Edward Island, on 25 June 1772. [PAPEI#2664/151]

MCINTYRE, NEIL, from Barra, emigrated aboard the brig <u>Alexander of Greenock</u> in June 1772, landed at Charlottetown, Prince Edward Island, on 25 June 1772. [PAPEI#2664/156]

MCINTYRE, RODERICK, from Barra, emigrated aboard the brig <u>Alexander of Greenock</u> in June 1772, landed at Charlottetown, Prince Edward Island, on 25 June 1772. [PAPEI#2664/151]

MCINTYRE, RORY, from Barra, emigrated aboard the brig <u>Alexander of Greenock</u> in June 1772, landed at Charlottetown, Prince Edward Island, on 25 June 1772. [PAPEI#2664/151]

MCKEE, DONALD, anad his wife, possibly from Moidart, emigrated aboard the brig <u>Alexander of Greenock</u> in June 1772, landed at Charlottetown, Prince Edward Island, on 25 June 1772. [SCA.BL.3/244/2]

MCKINNON, ALLAN, a carpenter from Barra, emigrated aboard the brig <u>Alexander of Greenock</u> in June 1772, landed at Charlottetown, Prince Edward Island, on 25 June 1772. [PAPEI#2664/148]

MCKINNON, ANGUS, from Boisdale, South Uist, emigrated aboard the brig <u>Alexander of Greenock</u> in June 1772, landed at Charlottetown, Prince Edward Island, on 25 June 1772. [PAPEI#2664/151]

MCKINNON, CHARLES, from Boisdale, South Uist, emigrated aboard the brig <u>Alexander of Greenock</u> in June 1772, landed at Charlottetown, Prince Edward Island, on 25 June 1772. [PAPEI#2664/151]

MCKINNON, LAUCHLAN, from Eigg, emigrated aboard the brig <u>Alexander of Greenock</u> in June 1772, landed at Charlottetown, Prince Edward Island, on 25 June 1772. [PAPEI#2664/151, 155]

MCLEOD, JOHN, from Glenfinnan, son of Murdoch McLeod of Harris, emigrated aboard the brig <u>Alexander of Greenock</u> in June 1772, landed at Charlottetown, Prince Edward Island, on 25 June 1772. [PAPEI#2664/145]

MCMILLAN, JOHN, from Boisdale, South Uist, emigrated aboard the brig <u>Alexander of Greenock</u> in June 1772, landed at Charlottetown, Prince Edward Island, on 25 June 1772. [PAPEI#2664/151]

MCMILLAN, JOHN, from Barra, emigrated aboard the brig <u>Alexander of Greenock</u> in June 1772, landed at Charlottetown, Prince Edward Island, on 25 June 1772. [PAPEI#2664/151]

MCNEIL, ANGUS, from Barra, emigrated aboard the brig <u>Alexander of Greenock</u> in June 1772, landed at Charlottetown, Prince Edward Island, on 25 June 1772. [PAPEI#2664/151]

Some passengers aboard the Pearl

CAMERON, ALEXANDER, born 1727 in Glenmoriston, Inverness-shire, from Fort William to New York aboard the <u>Pearl</u> in 1773, settled on the Kingsborough Patent, New York, a soldier of the Royal Regiment of New York from 1780 to 1783, moved to Cornwall, Ontario. [DFpp]

CAMERON, JOHN, born in Glenmoriston, Inverness-shire, from Fort William to New York aboard the <u>Pearl</u> in 1773, settled on the Kingsborough Patent, New York, moved to Cornwall, Ontario. [DFpp]

CAMERON, JOHN MCAFEE, born in Rannoch, Perth-shire, from Fort William to New York aboard the <u>Pearl</u> in 1773, settled on the Kingsborough Patent, New York, a soldier of the Royal Regiment of New York from 1776 to 1783, moved to Fairfield, Lancaster, Glengarry, Ontario. [DFpp]

CHISHOLM, ALEXANDER, from Fort William to New York aboard the Pearl in 1773, settled on the Kingsborough Patent, New York, a soldier of the Royal Regiment of New York, moved to Charlottenburg, Ontario. [DFpp]

CHISHOLM, ALEXANDER, settled on Johnson's Patent, Tryon County, New York, a Loyalist in 1776. [NA.AO13.11.C1]

CHISHOLM, ALEXANDER, a merchant in Ticonderoga, New York, by 1776, moved to Quebec by 1783 then to Montreal in 1781 [NA.AU13.11.C1]]

CHISHOLM, GEORGE, in Aesopus County, New York, a Loyalist in 1776, moved to Shelbourne, Nova Scotia, by 1786. [NA.AO13.25.19]

CHISHOLM, HUGH, settled on Johnston's Patent, Tryon County, New York, before 1776, moved to Quebec by 1786. [NA.AO13.11.C1]

CHISHOLM, JOHN, settled in Tryon County, New York, before 1776, moved to Niagara by 1786. [NA.AO13.11.C1]

CHISHOLM, WILLIAM, settled on Johnston's Patent, Tryon County, New York, before 1776, moved to New Johnstown, Canada. [NA.AO13.11.C1]

GRANT, DONALD, from Fort William to New York aboard the Pearl in 1773, settled on the Kingsborough Patent, New York, a soldier of the Royal Regiment of New York from 1776 to 1783, moved to Charlottenburg, Ontario. [DFpp]

GRANT, DONALD, a weaver from Croskey, from Fort William to New York aboard the Pearl in 1773, settled on the Kingsborough Patent, New York, a soldier of the Royal Regiment of New York, moved to Charlottenburg, Ontario. [DFpp]

GRANT, DUNCAN, from Fort William to New York aboard the Pearl in 1773, settled on the Kingsborough Patent, New York, a soldier of the Royal Regiment of New York, moved to Charlottenburg, Ontario. [DFpp]

GRANT, FINLAY, from Fort William to New York aboard the Pearl in 1773, settled on the Kingsborough Patent, New York, a soldier of the Royal Regiment of New York, moved to Charlottenburg, Ontario. [DFpp]

GRANT, JOHN, from Fort William to New York aboard the <u>Pearl</u> in 1773, settled on the Kingsborough Patent, New York, a soldier of the Royal Regiment of New York, died in Canada during 1777. [DFpp]

GRANT, PETER, from Fort William to New York aboard the <u>Pearl</u> in 1773, settled on the Kingsborough Patent, New York, a soldier of the Royal Regiment of New York, moved to Charlottenburg, Ontario. [DFpp]

MCDONALD, DONALD, from Fort William aboard the Pearl bound for New York in 1773, settled in Tryon County, New York, before 1776. [NA.AO12.29.74]

MCDONALD, RANDALL, settled on the Mohawk River, Tryon County, New York, by 1776. [NA.AO.12.28.23]

MCDONELL, ALEXANDER, from Boleskine, Stratherick, to America in 1773, settled on the Kingsborough Patent, New York, a soldier of the Royal Regiment of New York from 1776 to 1783, moved to the River Raison, Ontario. [DFpp] [NA.AO12.31.192]

MCDONELL, ALEXANDER, from Knoydart, Inverness-shire, to America in 1773, settled on the Kingsborough Patent, New York, a soldier of the 84th [Royal Highland Emigrants] Regiment, moved to Cornwall, Ontario. [DFpp] [NA.AO.13.14.93]

MCDONELL, ALEXANDER, from Aberchalder, Inverness-shire, from Fort William aboard the <u>Pearl</u> to New York in 1773, a Captain of the Royal Regiment of New York and of the 84th [Royal Highland Emigrant] Regiment, husband of ...... McDonell, moved to Glengarry, Ontario. [NA.AO13.80.289][DFpp]

MCDONELL, ALEXANDER, born 1762 at Fort Augustus, Inverness-shire, son of Allan McDonell and Helen Chisholm, to New York aboard the <u>Pearl</u> in 1773, a soldier of the 84th [Royal Highland Emigrant] Regiment and of Butler's Rangers, died in Toronto during 1842. [DFpp]

MCDONELL, ALLAN, born 1712 son of Alexander McDonell in Collachie, Loch Oich, Inverness-shire, a Jacobite in 1745, an officer in the French Army, from Fort William to New York aboard the <u>Pearl</u> in 1773, settled at Soharie, Tryon County, on the Kingsborough Patent, a Captain of the 84th [Royal Highland Emigrant] Regiment, moved to Quebec in 1779, married Helen McNab, parents of Angus, Alexander, James, Henrietta, and Catherine, died at Cap Rouge, Quebec, during 1792, buried at St Foy. [DFpp][NA.AO12.27.396]

MCDONELL, ALLEN, from Fort William to New York aboard the Pearl in 1773, settled on the Kingsborough Patent, a soldier of the Royal Regiment of New York from 1776 to 1783, moved to Charlottenburg, Ontario. [DFpp]

MCDONELL, ANGUS, from Fort William to New York aboard the Pearl in 1773, settled on the Kingsborough Patent, New York, a soldier of the 84th [Royal Highland Emigrant] Regiment, later moved to Cornwall, Ontario.[DFpp][NA.AO13.8.228]

MCDONELL, ARCHIBALD, to New York aboard the Pearl in 1773, settled on the Kingsborough Patent, New York, a Lieutenant of the 84th [Royal Highland Emigrant] Regiment. [DFpp]

MCDONELL, DONALD, from Kilmorack, Inverness-shire, to New York aboard the Pearl in 1773, a Corporal of the 84th [Royal Highland Emigrant] Regiment, moved to Charlottenburg, Ontario. [DFpp]

MCDONELL, DONALD, from Glenmoriston, Inverness-shire, from Fort William to New York aboard the Pearl in 1773, settled on the Kingsborough Patent, New York, a soldier of the 2nd Battalion of the Royal Regiment of New York from 1780 to 1783, moved to Cornwall, Ontario. [DFpp]

MCDONELL, DUNCAN, from Fort William to New York aboard the Pearl in 1773, settled in Tryon County, New York, a Loyalist in 1776. [DFpp][NA.AO12.31.147]

MCDONELL, HUGH, to New York aboard the Pearl in 1773, settled in Tryon County, New York, a Loyalist in 1776. [NA.AO12.29.103]

MCDONELL, JOHN, from Inveroucht, Inverness-shire, from Fort William to New York aboard the Pearl in 1773, settled on the Kingsborough Patent, New York, a soldier of the 2nd Battalion of the Royal Regiment of New York from 1780 to 1783, moved to River Raison, Ontario. [DFpp][NA.AO12.31.179]

MCDONELL, JOHN, from Dalchreggan, Inverness-shire, from Fort William to New York aboard the Pearl in 1773, settled on the Kingsborough Patent, New

York, a soldier of the 1st Battalion of the Royal Regiment of New York, moved to Canada. [DFpp]

MCDONELL, JOHN, from Collachie, Inverness-shire, from Fort William to New York aboard the Pearl in 1773, settled on the Kingsborough Patent, New York, a soldier of the 1st Battalion of the 84th [Royal Highland Emigrant] Regiment from 1776 to 1783, moved to Ontario. [DFpp][NA.AO12.28.401]

MCDONELL, JOHN, from Leek, Loch Oich, Inverness-shire, a Jacobite in 1745, an officer of the 78th Regiment during the French and Indian Wars, returned to Scotland, from Fort William to New York aboard the Pearl in 1773, settled on the Kingsborough Patent, New York, husband of Jean Magdalena Chisholm, Captain of the 84th [Royal Highland Emigrant] Regiment, moved to Canada, died in Montreal on 11 November 1782. [DFpp][PCCol.V.597][NA.AO13.80.288]

MCDONELL, JOHN, from Baldron, Inverness-shire, from Fort William to New York aboard the Pearl in 1773, settled on the Kingsborough Patent, New York, a soldier of the Royal Regiment of New York, moved to Charlottenburg, Ontario. [DFpp]

MCDONELL, JOHN, from Fort Augustus, Inverness-shire, from Fort William to New York aboard the Pearl in 1773, settled on the Kingsborough Patent, New York, a soldier of the Royal Regiment of New York, died in 1786. [DFpp]

MCDONELL, JOHN, from Aughengleen, Inverness-shire, from Fort William to New York aboard the Pearl in 1773, settled on the Kingsborough Patent, New York, a soldier of the 84th [Royal Highland Emigrant] Regiment from 1776 to 1783, moved to New Johnstown, Ontario. [DFpp][NA.AO12.29.242]

MCDONELL, JOHN ROY, from Fort William to New York aboard the Pearl in 1773, settled on the Kingsborough Patent, New York, a soldier of the 84th [Royal Highland Emigrant] Regiment, from 1776 to 1783, moved to Glengarry, Canada. [DFpp]

MCDONELL, KENNETH, from Fort William to New York aboard the Pearl in 1773, settled on the Kingsborough Patent, New York, a soldier of the 84th [Royal Highland Emigrant] Regiment, from 1776 to 1783, moved to Cornwall, Ontario. [DFpp][NA.AO12.31.49]

MCDONELL, MILES, born 1767 in Inverness, from Fort William to New York aboard the Pearl in 1773, settled in Tryon County, New York, moved to Canada, an officer of the Royal Canadian Volunteers, later from 1811 to 1820 in Hudson Bay Company Service, died at Port Fortune on the Ottawa River on 28 June 1828. [HBRA.2.232]

MCDONELL, RANOLD, fought in the French and Indian Wars, returned to Scotland, from Fort William to New York aboard the Pearl in 1773, settled on the Kingsborough Patent, New York, moved to Cornwall, Ontario, in 1783. [DFpp]

MCDONELL, RODERICK, from Glenmoriston, Inverness-shire, from Fort William to New York aboard the Pearl in 1773, settled on the Kingsborough Patent, New York, a soldier of the Royal Regiment of New York from 1776 to 1783, moved to Charlottenburg, Ontario. [DFpp][NA.AO12.28.390]

MCDOUGALL, JOHN, from Fort William to New York aboard the Pearl in 1773, settled in Argyle, Charlotte County, New York. [NA.AO12.29.230]

MCGRUER, DONALD, from Fort William aboard the Pearl to America in 1773, a farmer at Johnson's Bush, Kingsborough Patent, New York, a soldier of the 84th [Royal Highland Emigrants] Regiment, died at Sorel in 1781. [DFpp][NA.AO12.29.252]

MCGRUER, JOHN, born in Boleskine, Abertarff, Inverness-shire, from Fort William aboard the Pearl to America in 1773, settled on the Kingsborough Patent, New York, a corporal of Royal Regiment of New York, moved to Charlottenburg, Ontario. [DFpp][NA.AO12.29.49]

MCINTOSH, JOHN, from Fort William aboard the Pearl to America in 1773, a farmer at Johnson's Bush, Kingsborough Patent, New York, a soldier of the 84th [Royal Highland Emigrants] Regiment from 1776 to 1783, moved to Riviere aux Raisins, Ontario. [DFpp]

MCKAY, DONALD, from Fort William aboard the Pearl to America in 1773, settled on the Kingsborough Patent, New York, a soldier of the Royal Regiment of New York, husband of Elspeth Kennedy, moved to Riviere aux Raisins, Ontario. [DFpp][NA.AO12.29.150]

MCLEAN, DUNCAN, from Fort William to New York aboard the Pearl in 1773, settled on the Kingsborough Patent, New York, a sergeant of the Royal Regiment of New York from 1776 to 1783, moved to Charlottenburg, Ontario. [DFpp][NA.AO12.27.194]

MCLEAN, MURDOCH, Fort William to New York aboard the Pearl in 1773, settled on the Kingsborough Patent, New York, a sergeant of the Royal Regiment of New York from 1776 to 1783, moved to Charlottenburg, Ontario. [DFpp][NA.AO12.27.194]

MCLEOD, WILLIAM, from Fort William to New York aboard the Pearl in 1773, settled on the Kingsborough Patent, New York, a Lieutenant of the Royal Regiment of New York from 1776 to 1783, moved to Charlottenburg, Ontario. [DFpp]

MCMULLEN, DONALD, from Fort William to New York aboard the Pearl in 1773, settled on the Kingsborough Patent, New York, moved to River Aux Raisins, Ontario. [DFpp]]

MCPHERSON, ALEXANDER, from Fort William to New York aboard the Pearl in 1773, settled on the Kingsborough Patent, New York, a soldier of the Royal Regiment of New York from 1776 to 1783, moved to Edwardsburgh, Grenville County, Ontario. [DFpp]

MCPHERSON, JAMES, from Fort William to New York aboard the Pearl in 1773, settled at Scotch Bush on the Kingsborough Patent, New York, moved to Canada after 1783. [NA.AO13.14.226]

MCPHERSON, LAUCHLAN, from Fort William to New York aboard the Pearl in 1773, settled on the Kingsborough Patent, New York, a soldier of the Royal Regiment of New York. [DFpp]

MCPHERSON, MURDOCH, from Fort William to New York aboard the Pearl in 1773, settled on the Kingsborough Patent, New York, a soldier of the Royal Regiment of New York from 1776 to 1783, moved to Charlottenburg, Ontario. [DFpp][NA.AO12.29.179]

MCPHERSON, WILLIAM, from Fort William to New York aboard the Pearl in 1773, settled on the Kingsborough Patent, New York. [DFpp]

Passengers, from Clanranald's lands, aboard the _Jane_ from Drimindarach to Prince Edward Island in 1790. [Source SCA. Oban papers]

ADAMSON, DONALD, a pedlar from Moidart, and wife.

CAMPBELL, JOHN, and family, from Island Shona.

GILLIES, DUNCAN, and family from Duchaniss.

GILLIES, WILLIAM, tenant in Tray, South Morar.

GRANT, DONALD, and family from Kenleod.

MCDONALD, ANABELLA, from Ardnafuaran.

MCDONALD, EWAN, tenant in Retland, South Morar, and family.

MACDONALD, JOHN, and family, from Scamdale, South Morar.

MCDONALD, JOHN, from Ardnafuaran, and family.

MCDONALD, JOHN, tenant in Slockkardnish, and family.

MCDONALD, JOHN, tenant in Slockkardnish.

MCDONALD, LAUCHLAN, and wife, from Ardgasrig.

MCDONALD, LUDOVICK, a tenant in Sauanister, Morar, and family.

MCDONALD, MARY, from Ardnafuaran.

MCDONALD, RANALD, from Retland, South Morar, and family.

MCEACHEN, DONALD, tenant in Slockkardnish, and family.

MCGILLVRAY, ANGUS, from Airnapoul, and family.

MCGILLVRAY, JOHN, and family from Mamy, and family.

MCGILLVRAY, JOHN, jr., and family, from Mamy.

MCGILLVRAY, WILLIAM, tenant in Mamy, and family.

MCKINNON, ALEXANDER, from Ardgasrig.

MCKINNON, MARION, from Ardgasrig.

Passengers, from Clanranald's lands, aboard the Lucy from Drimindarach to Prince Edward Island in 1790. [Source SCA. Oban papers]

ADAMSON, ALEXANDER, a tenant and family from Glenuig

ADAMSON, LAUCHLAN, a tenant with family from Glenuig

CHISHOLM, ALEXANDER, and family, from Kenleod

CORBET, ALEXANDER, a carpenter

MCDONALD, ALEXANDER, a tenant and family from Glenuig

MCDONALD, ALEXANDER, a pedlar and family, from Galmistle, Isle of Egg

MCDONALD, ANGUS, and family, from Houlun, Isle of Egg

MCDONALD, ANN, with family, from Isle Shona, Moidart

MCDONALD, DONALD, with family, from Isle Shona, Moidart

MCDONALD, DONALD, a tenant and family from Arienskill

MCDONALD, DONALD, and family, from Kentra, Moidart

MCDONALD, JOHANA, from Samlaman

MCDONALD, JOHN, and family, from Borrodale

MCDONALD, JOHN, a tenant and family, from Glenuig

MCDONALD, LAUCHLAN, and family, from Essan

MCDONALD, RODERICK, and wife from Kyles

MCEACHUN, ALEXANDER, a tenant and wife from Arienskill

MCEACHUN, ANGUS, a smith and family from Arienskill

MCEACHUN, JOHN, (1), with family, from Isle Shona, Moidart

MCEACHUN, JOHN, (2), from Isle Shona, Moidart

MCEACHUN, JOHN, (3), with family from Kenochailort

MCGILLVRAY, DONALD, a carpenter and wife from Kyles

MCINTYRE, JOHN, a tenant, and wife, from Kyles

MCINRYE, DONALD, tenant from Kyles

MCISAAC, KATHERINE, with family from Isle Shona, Moidart

MCISAAC, PEGGY, from Isle Shona, Moidart

MCKELLAIG, DONALD, from Irin

MCKELLAIG, MARY, and family, from Kyles, South Morar

MCLEAN, JOHN, a tenant and family, from Kildounain

MCMILLAN, ALEXANDER, and family from Toray

MCMILLAN, DONALD, a tenant and family from Kincreggan

MCMILLAN, DUNCAN, a tenant and family from Arienskill

MCMILLAN, JOHN, a tenant and wife from Kincreggan

MACPHERSON, JOHN, a tenant from Kyles

Passengers, from Clanranald's lands, aboard the _British Queen_ from Arisaig to Quebec in 1790. [Source Public Archives of Canada, RG4A1, vol.48, fos.15874-5]

CAMPBELL, LACHLAN, and family, from Easdale, Egg

FRASER, DONALD, a smith and family, from Ardnafouran, Arisaig

GILLIES, DUNCAN, a tenant and family, from Ronasick, North Morar

GILLIS, JOHN, a tenant and family, from Beorarrd, North Morar

HENDERSON, DONALD, a servant from Invergosurn, Knoydart

MCAULAY, DONALD, a smith and family, from Trobert, South Uist

MCAULAY, JOHN, a servant from Frobart, South Uist

MCCARMICH, DONALD, (1), a tenant and child, from Easdale, Egg

MCCARMICH, DONALD, (2), from Easdale, Egg

MCCRAE, DUNCAN, a servant, from Invergosurn, Knoydart

MCDONALD, ALLAN, and family, from Cleadle, Egg

MCDONALD, DONALD, a tenant and family from Cleadale, Egg

MCDONALD, DONALD, a tenant from Easdale, Egg

MCDONALD, DONALD, a tenant and family, from Laganachdrum, Glengarry

MCDONALD, JANET, a servant

MCDONNELL, JOHN, a tenant and family, from Invergosurn, Knoydart

MCDOUGAL, PEGGY, and child, from Cleadale, Egg

MCKAY, JOHN, a tenant from Ardnafouran, Arisaig

MCKINNON, JOHN, a tenant from Cleadale, Egg

MCKINNON, LACHLAN, a tenant and family from Easdale, Egg

MCLELLAN, ANGUS, a tailor and family, from Lagannachrum, Glengarry

MCMILLAN, DOUGALD, a tenant and family, from Drumulu, Moidart

MCMILLAN, EWAN, a tenant and family from Laidnaset, Ardgour